T0318995

Cambridge Elements ≡

Elements in the Philosophy of Religion
edited by
Yujin Nagasawa
University of Birmingham

ATHEISM AND AGNOSTICISM

Graham Oppy
Monash University, Victoria

CAMBRIDGE
UNIVERSITY PRESS

CAMBRIDGE
UNIVERSITY PRESS

University Printing House, Cambridge CB2 8BS, United Kingdom

One Liberty Plaza, 20th Floor, New York, NY 10006, USA

477 Williamstown Road, Port Melbourne, VIC 3207, Australia

314–321, 3rd Floor, Plot 3, Splendor Forum, Jasola District Centre,
New Delhi – 110025, India

79 Anson Road, #06–04/06, Singapore 079906

Cambridge University Press is part of the University of Cambridge.

It furthers the University's mission by disseminating knowledge in the pursuit of
education, learning, and research at the highest international levels of excellence.

www.cambridge.org
Information on this title: www.cambridge.org/9781108454728
DOI: 10.1017/9781108555340

First published 2018

A catalogue record for this publication is available from the British Library.

ISBN 978-1-108-45472-8 Paperback
ISSN 2399-5165 (online)
ISSN 2515-9763 (print)

Atheism and Agnosticism

Graham Oppy

Abstract: *This Element is an elementary introduction to atheism and agnosticism. It begins with a careful characterisation of atheism and agnosticism, distinguishing them from many other things with which they are often conflated. After a brief discussion of the theoretical framework within which atheism and agnosticism are properly evaluated, the Element then turns to the sketching of cases for atheism and agnosticism. In both cases, the aim is not conviction, but rather advancement of understanding: the point of the cases is to make it intelligible why some take themselves to have compelling reason to adopt atheism or agnosticism.*

Keywords: *Agnosticism, Atheism, Big Pictures, Causation, Design, Divination, Experience, Mind, Scripture, Theoretical Virtues*

Issns: 2399-5165 (online), 2515-9763 (print)
Isbns: 9781108454728 PB, 9781108555340 OC

1 Introduction

Atheists and agnostics get lots of bad press. For many years, atheists and agnostics have been the most disliked – despised and distrusted – minority in the United States. According to Edgell et al. (2006), 40 per cent of Americans maintain that atheists and agnostics do not fit into their vision of American society, and 48 per cent would disapprove if their child married an atheist or an agnostic. Interestingly, while *some* Americans associate atheism and agnosticism with illegal behaviour such as drug use and prostitution – threatening 'respectable society' from the 'lower end' of the social ladder – *others* associate atheism and agnosticism with rampant materialism and cultural elitism – threatening 'respect-able society' by way of 'upper end' ostentatious consumption and intellectual snobbery. According to Edgell et al. (2006:230):

> Americans construct the atheist [and the agnostic] as the symbolic representation of one who rejects the basis for moral solidarity and cultural membership in American society altogether.

While atheists and agnostics can 'pass' in American society – it is, after all, impossible to identify atheists and agnostics who give no public expression to their views – many people treat atheists and agnostics as scapegoats for perceived social ills at both ends of the social ladder.

In the less recent past, atheists and agnostics got much worse than bad press. For example, the 1661 UK Act against the Crime of Blasphemy made it a capital offence to 'obstinately persist' in denial of the existence of God: under this Act, atheists and agnostics could be put to death merely for giving ongoing verbal expression to their convictions. Because blasphemy encompasses much more than mere persistent denial of the existence of God, and because it is unclear whether there were unreported cases, we do not know whether anyone in the UK was sanctioned – by fine, corporal punishment, imprisonment, or capital punishment – merely for persistent denial of the existence of God. Moreover, by the mid-nineteenth century, while statutes continued to forbid public denial of the existence of God, it was established legal opinion that only behaviour that tended to subvert society merited legal sanction, and that mere public denial of the existence of God was not behaviour that tended to subvert society. Nonetheless, UK blasphemy laws had a chilling effect on the freedom of speech of atheists and agnostics until well into the twentieth century.

Some parts of the world remain inhospitable to atheists and agnostics. As Ohlheiser (2013) reports, there are many countries – including Afghanistan, Iran, Maldives, Mauritania, Nigeria, Pakistan, Qatar, Saudi Arabia, Somalia, Sudan, United Arab Emirates, and Yemen – where the law allows for atheists and agnostics to be put to death simply for their persistent denial of the existence of gods. Moreover, in these, and many other, countries, there have been vigilante attacks on those officially branded 'atheists' and 'agnostics'. In Bangladesh, in the past five years, 'atheist bloggers' Niloy Chakrabarti, Ananta Bijoy Das, Faisal Arefin Dipan, Ahmed Rajib Haider, Washiqur Rahman, and Arijit Roy have all died in religiously motivated machete attacks. While there are parts of the world where atheists and agnostics do not get more bad press than other minority groups, there are few places where atheists and agnostics are not routinely publicly denounced by religious leaders. Even in the most secular states – such as Australia, the Czech Republic, France, Germany, Japan, the Netherlands, Sweden, the United Kingdom, and Vietnam – it is not uncommon for religious leaders to attack the decency, integrity, probity, rationality, and virtue of atheists and agnostics.

Given the widespread scapegoating of atheists and agnostics – both in the past and the present – it is unsurprising that atheism and agnosticism are widely misunderstood. Because the words 'atheist' and 'agnostic' are frequently used as slurs and terms of abuse, these words are often used without any understanding of the shared attitudes of those who self-identify as atheists or agnostics. The first task, in any investigation of atheism and agnosticism, is to get clear about the meanings of the terms that are to be used in that investigation. This task is partly stipulative: I shall say how these words are to be understood, and why it is good to understand these words in this way. But the task is constrained by the ways that we all speak: it should not seem to you that the meanings that are being given to these words are merely figments of my imagination.

1.1 Atheists and Agnostics

The defining features of atheists and agnostics – i.e. the features whose possession make people atheists and agnostics – are their attitudes towards the claim that *there are no gods*.

Atheists believe that there are no gods. Hence, in suitable circumstances, atheists affirm that there are no gods and endorse the claim that there are no gods.

Agnostics suspend judgement on the claim that there are no gods. Agnostics neither believe that there are gods, nor believe that there are no gods, despite having given consideration to the question whether there are gods.

Agnostics are distinguished from *innocents*, who also neither believe that there are gods nor believe that there are no gods, by the fact that they have given consideration to the question whether there are gods. Innocents are those who have never considered the question whether there are gods. Typically, innocents have never considered the question whether there are gods because they are not able to consider that question. How could that be? Well, in order to consider the question whether there are gods, one must understand what it would mean for something to be a god. That is, one needs to have the *concept* of a god. Those who lack the concept of a god are not able to entertain the thought that there are gods. Consider, for example, one-month-old babies. It is very plausible that one-month-old babies lack the concept of a god. So it is very plausible that one-month-old babies are innocents. Other plausible cases of innocents include chimpanzees, human beings who have suffered severe traumatic brain injuries, and human beings with advanced dementia.

1.2   Gods

Our characterisations of atheism and agnosticism mention gods. What are gods? Roughly: gods are sufficiently highly ranked supernatural beings or forces that have and exercise power over the natural world. Why 'roughly'? Because 'sufficiently highly ranked' is vague. It is sometimes said that gods are not under the power of higher-ranking beings and forces. But, for example, in Greek mythology, the gods are subject to the fates. I shall not try to give a more precise definition of 'god'; instead, I shall rely on your prior understanding of this term, which is based upon familiar examples: Aztec gods, Celtic gods, Chinese gods, Greek gods, Hawaiian gods, Hindu gods, Incan gods, Inuit gods, Japanese gods, Korean gods, Maori gods, Mesopotamian gods, Norse gods, Roman gods, Semitic gods, Yoruba gods, and so on.

Theists are those who believe that *there is at least one god*. The defining belief of atheists and the defining belief of theists are contradictories: one is true exactly if the other is false.

Monotheists are theists who have the further belief that *there is no more than one god*. Equivalently, monotheists believe that *there is exactly one god*. Monotheists who believe that there is exactly one god typically accept that the god in which they believe is properly called 'God'. So, more or less equivalently, monotheists believe that *God exists*.

Polytheists are theists who have the further belief that *there is not exactly one god*. Equivalently, polytheists believe that *there is more than one god*. Given the defining belief of theists, the defining belief of monotheists and the defining belief of polytheists are contradictories.

One important point to note is that, while it is true that atheists believe that God does not exist, this is not the defining feature of atheists. What makes someone an atheist is that they believe that there are *no* gods. It is merely a consequence of this fundamental commitment that atheists claim that God does not exist.

Another important point to note is that it *may* be that some agnostics believe that God does not exist. The defining feature of agnostics is that they suspend judgement on the question whether there are gods. It is consistent with one's suspending judgement on the question whether there are gods that one believes that there is not exactly one god, so long as one suspends judgement on the question whether there is more than one god. Perhaps it would be odd for an agnostic to believe that God does not exist, but it is clearly conceivable that there may be someone who has this combination of attitudes.

Some people relativise atheism to particular gods or particular classes of gods. Such people say that a person is an atheist with respect to a given god, no matter what attitudes that person has to other gods. So, for example, these people say that Christians are atheists with respect to the Norse gods. This way of talking is misguided: no one says that a person is a vegan with respect to those occasions on which they sit down to a meal that contains no animal products.

As we have already noted, an agnostic is someone who does not believe in any gods, but who suspends judgement on the existence of at least one god. Thus, for any particular gods, it is a further question whether an agnostic suspends judgement about those particular gods. Similarly, for any particular gods, it is a further question whether a theist believes in those particular gods. Nonetheless, we do nothing but invite confusion if we relativise theism and agnosticism to particular classes of gods. Theists believe in some gods but may fail to believe in others. Agnostics suspend judgement on some gods but may disbelieve in others.

1.3 Isms

Atheism is the position that is adopted by atheists. Atheism is characterised by the claim that there are no gods. *Atheistic* theories – or worldviews, or big pictures – include or entail the claim that there are no gods.

Agnosticism is the position that is adopted by agnostics. Agnosticism is characterised by suspension of judgement on the claim that there are no gods. *Agnostic* theories – or worldviews, or big pictures – give consideration to the question whether there are gods, but include or entail *neither* the claim that there are no gods *nor* the claim that there is at least one god.

Theism is the view that is adopted by theists. Theism is characterised by the claim that there is at least one god. *Theistic* theories – or worldviews, or big pictures – include or entail that claim that there is at least one god. *Monotheistic* theories – or worldviews or big pictures – include or entail the claim that God exists.

Polytheistic theories – or worldviews or big pictures – include or entail the claim that there is more than one god.

Atheism and theism are contradictories: one is true exactly if the other is false. Atheistic theories and theistic theories are *contraries*: at most, one of any given pair of an atheistic theory and a theistic theory is true, though, often enough, both members of the pair are false.

1.4　Qualities of Belief

The characterisation of atheism and agnosticism says nothing about the *qualities* of the beliefs of atheists and agnostics.

There is a spectrum of *degree* of conviction for atheists. Some atheists are *certain* that there are no gods, some atheists believe with only *the least degree* of conviction that there are no gods, and other atheists occupy all points in between. If we suppose that people have credences – i.e. they assign probabilities to propositions – then we can assume the following: some atheists have a credence of 100 per cent for the claim that there are no gods, some atheists have a credence just above 50 per cent for the claim that there are no gods, and other atheists have credences distributed throughout the range that lies above 50 per cent and below 100 per cent.

There is also a spectrum of *robustness* of conviction for atheists. Some atheists are *fixed* in their attitudes to – and their credences for – the claim that there are no gods; some atheists are not at all fixed in their attitudes to – and their credences for – the claim that there are no gods; and other atheists occupy all points in between.

While there is not a spectrum of degree of conviction for agnostics – if we suppose that people have credences, then agnostics are those who assign a credence of precisely 50 per cent to the claim that there are no gods – there is a spectrum of robustness of conviction for agnostics. Some agnostics are fixed in their attitudes to – and their credence for – the claim that there are no gods; some agnostics are not at all fixed in their attitudes to – and their credence for – the claim that there are no gods; and other agnostics occupy all points in between.

The range of qualities of belief is the same for atheists and agnostics as it is for theists: some are dogmatic, opinionated, peremptory, and doctrinaire; some are tentative and open-minded; and others fall at all points in between.

1.5   Other Attitudes

The characterisation of atheism and agnosticism says nothing about other attitudes that atheists and agnostics take towards the claim that defines their positions.

Some atheists and agnostics *want* it to be that there is at least one god; often enough, they want it to be that some particular god exists, or that some particular gods exist. Some atheists and agnostics want it to be that there are no gods. Some atheists and agnostics neither want it to be that there is at least one god nor want it to be that there are no gods; these atheists and agnostics are, in a certain sense, indifferent to the existence of gods. Of course, this is not to say that these atheists and agnostics are indifferent to the existence of *each* particular god; it is very likely that almost all atheists and agnostics, along with almost all theists, want it to be that some particular gods do not exist. I expect that most people alive today would want it to be the case that Sekhmet does not exist.

There is a spectrum of *interest* in the question whether there is at least one god. Some atheists and agnostics care deeply whether there is at least one god. Some atheists and agnostics have no interest in thinking about – let alone arguing about – whether there is at least one god. Other atheists and agnostics occupy all points in between. Theists are distributed right across this same spectrum. Some – see, for example, Rauch (2003), Phipps (2013), von Hegner (2016) – have wanted to introduce a new term – *apatheist* – for those at the disinterested end of this spectrum; it's hard to believe that the new term will pay its way.

Some monotheists – in particular, Abrahamic monotheists – who believe that God exists also claim to have *faith* in God, where this faith in God is something more than either hope or belief that God exists. Despite frequently encountered claims to the contrary, there is no counterpart to this faith on the part of atheists and agnostics. It is true that, for a great many things, atheists and agnostics believe that there are those things: atoms, molecules, paramecia, snakes, car, cities, oceans, planets, galaxies, and so forth. But no one – theist, atheist, or agnostic – has faith in those things. To think otherwise is to make a mistake about what it means to have faith in God.

1.6 Disagreement

The characterisation of atheism and agnosticism says nothing about the attitudes that atheists and agnostics take towards those who *disagree* with the stances that atheists and agnostics take towards the claim that defines their positions.

Some atheists maintain that, in virtue of their agnosticism or theism, all agnostics and theists are *irrational*. Some agnostics maintain that, in virtue of their atheism or theism, all atheists and theists are irrational. Some theists maintain that, in virtue of their atheism or agnosticism, all atheists and agnostics are irrational.

Some atheists maintain that no agnostics or theists are *sufficiently well-informed* about matters that bear on the claim that there are no gods. Some agnostics maintain that no atheists or theists are sufficiently well-informed about matters that bear on the claim that there are no gods. Some theists maintain that no atheists or agnostics are sufficiently well-informed on matters that bear on the claim that there are no gods.

Some atheists maintain that all *thoughtful, reflective, sufficiently intelligent, sufficiently well-informed* people who give serious attention to the matter believe that there are no gods. Some agnostics maintain that *thoughtful, reflective, sufficiently intelligent, sufficiently well-informed* people who give serious attention to the matter suspend judgement on the question whether there are any gods. Some theists maintain that all *thoughtful, reflective, sufficiently intelligent, sufficiently well-informed* people who give serious attention to the matter believe that there is at least one god.

Some atheists maintain that agnostics and theists can reasonably disagree with them about whether there are any gods. Some agnostics maintain that atheists and theists can reasonably disagree with them about whether there are any gods. Some theists maintain that atheists and agnostics can reasonably disagree with them about whether there are any gods.

There is nothing *intrinsic* to atheism, or agnosticism, or theism, that makes it more likely that proponents of one of these positions will be more – or less – *dismissive* of opposing positions than proponents of the other two positions. There is nothing intrinsic to atheism, or agnosticism, or theism that makes it more likely that proponents of one of these positions will be more – or less – angry, arrogant, conceited, defensive, hostile, insincere, meretricious, militant, opinionated, passive-aggressive, prejudiced, rude, sanctimonious, shallow, superficial, tactless, or vindictive than proponents of the other two positions.

1.7 Knowledge

Some people have suggested that agnosticism requires not merely suspension of judgement on whether there are gods, but also commitment to the further claim that it is *unknown* – or perhaps even *unknowable* – whether there are gods. (In the coming discussion, I shall rely on the familiar – but not uncontested – philosophical claim that knowledge is warranted true belief: a person knows a proposition just in case (a) the proposition is true, (b) the person believes the proposition, and (c) the person is warranted in believing the proposition.)

It seems wrong to suggest that agnostics endorse the claim that it is unknowable whether there are gods. Plausibly, if there are gods, then, for all we know, it is possible for them to make their existence known to us. But if it is possible for gods to make their existence known to us, then it is possible for us to know that there are gods.

So agnostics cannot coherently suppose that it is unknowable whether there are gods. Rather, agnostics should also suspend judgement on the question whether it is knowable that there are gods.

It also seems wrong to suggest that agnostics endorse the claim that it is unknown whether there are gods. Plausibly, if there are gods, then, for all we know, it may be that the gods have made their existence known to some of us. But, if gods have made their existence known to some of us, then their existence is not unknown. While it may be that agnostics can coherently suppose that it is unknown whether there are gods, it would seem more consonant with the agnostic's view to suspend judgement on the question whether it is known that there are gods.

None of this is to say that there are no constraints on what atheists, agnostics, and theists can say about what is known – or knowable – concerning the existence of gods. For example: an atheist who considers the claim must accept that *no one knows that there are gods*; and an atheist who considers the claim must accept that *no one knows that it is unknowable whether there are gods*; and an atheist who consider the claim must accept that *no one knows that it is unknown whether there are gods*.

Consider just the last case. Suppose that an atheist believes that *someone knows that it is unknown whether there are gods*. Then that atheist believes – or can infer from what they believe – that *it is unknown whether there are gods*. But the atheist believes that there are no gods. So that atheist believes – or can infer – that they do not have warrant for their belief that there are no gods: if they had warrant for that belief, then they would know that there are no gods, and so would know whether there are gods. But, once the atheist recognises that their belief that there are no gods is unwarranted, the atheist also recognises that their belief that there are no gods is defeated: they themselves do not have adequate reason to go on believing that there are no gods. And so the atheist will have to give up their belief that there are no gods in order to reasonably maintain the belief that someone knows that it is unknown whether there are gods. (Of course, one can be an atheist without considering *any* of the claims introduced in the preceding paragraph.)

1.8 Proof

Some people have supposed that atheism requires commitment to the claim that it has been *proven* that there are no gods. For consistency, these people doubtless suppose that theism requires commitment to the claim that it has been proven that there is at least one god, and that anyone who is committed, both to the claim that it has not been proven that there are no gods and to the claim that it has not been proven that there is at least one god, is an agnostic.

In order to assess this standpoint, we need to be clear about what would constitute a *proof*. In the formal sciences – mathematics, logic, statistics, game theory, and so forth – a proof is a derivation from a set of uncontested premises, i.e. from a set of premises upon which there is universal expert consensus. It is not controversial to observe that, by these standards, we have no proof that there are no gods, and no proof that there is at least one god. Given this standard of proof, everyone who is not an innocent should be an agnostic.

Perhaps it might be proposed that, for a given person, a proof is a derivation from a set of premises that *that* person – and any person of like mind – accepts. By this standard, it is uncontroversial that any person with sufficient logical acumen can construct proofs for any claims that they accept. But making the classification depend upon whether people *actually have* constructed proofs would be perverse; and allowing classification to proceed on the basis of the *availability* of proofs would remove all content from the requirement.

The idea that belief requires proof is connected to the idea that belief requires certainty. Inevitably, adoption of this requirement – in connection with subject matters that do not fall within the formal sciences – leads either to unbridled dogmatism concerning that subject matter or else to universal suspension of judgement concerning that subject matter. Insistence on a reasonable fallibilism in connection with believing militates against accepting that belief requires proof for any domains that fall outside the formal sciences.

Hence, we should reject the suggestion that atheism requires commitment to the claim that it has been *proven* that there are no gods.

1.9   Other Isms

While atheism and agnosticism are defined in terms of doxastic attitudes towards the claim that there are no gods, there are other claims that are routinely – but mistakenly – attributed to atheists and agnostics.

Naturalism is the view that (a) there are none but natural entities with none but natural causal powers, and (b) well-established science is the touchstone for identifying causal entities and causal powers. Since gods are non-natural causal entities with non-natural causal powers that are not postulated or identified in any well-established science, naturalists are atheists: naturalists hold that that are no gods. However, not all atheists are naturalists: there are atheists who believe that there are non-natural causal entities with non-natural causal powers, but that these non-natural causal entities with non-natural causal powers are not gods. Agnostics cannot be naturalists; at best, agnostics suspend judgement on the question whether there are non-natural causal entities with non-natural causal powers.

Physicalism is the view that (a) there are none but physical entities with none but physical causal powers, and (b) well-established science is the touchstone for identifying causal entities and causal powers. *Materialism* is the view that (a) there are none but material entities with none but material causal powers, and (b) well-established science is the touchstone for identifying causal entities and causal powers. What holds for naturalism holds also for physicalism and materialism. Physicalists are atheists, but not all atheists are physicalists. Materialists are atheists, but not all atheists are materialists. Agnostics cannot be physicalists; at best, agnostics suspend judgement on the question whether there are non-physical causal entities with non-physical causal powers. Agnostics cannot be materialists; at best, agnostics suspend judgement on the question whether there are non-material causal entities with non-material causal powers.

Scepticism, as I shall understand it here, is the claim that there is very little that we are rationally justified in believing. In particular, scepticism entails that there is very little that we are rationally justified in believing about the external world, other minds, the extent of the past, morality, modality, meaning, and so on. Given that scepticism recommends suspension of judgement about almost everything, it is unsurprising that sceptics are agnostics. But, of course, very few agnostics are sceptics; agnostics typically suspend judgement on the question whether there are gods against the background of belief in a vast range of claims about the external world, other minds, the extent of the past, morality, modality, meaning, and so on. Atheists are not sceptics; given that atheists believe that there are no gods, it is unsurprising that this atheistic belief sits in vast networks of beliefs about the external world, other minds, the extent of the past, morality, modality, meaning, and so on.

It is sometimes said that atheists are *evaluative nihilists* who maintain that nothing has any value, and that agnostics are *evaluative sceptics* who suspend judgement on the question whether some things have value. While it is plausible that most evaluative nihilists are atheists and that most evaluative sceptics are agnostics, there are many atheists who are not evaluative nihilists, and there are many agnostics who are not evaluative sceptics. Atheists and agnostics typically think that it is *wrong* to sexually abuse young children, *laudable* to speak out against hypocrisy, *commendable* to work for famine relief, and so on. Perhaps, at least locally, there are significant differences between atheists, agnostics, and theists in what they value; but it is one thing for someone to have values that are different from one's own, and quite another thing for someone to have no values at all.

1.10 Misconceptions

Some people say that atheism and agnosticism are *religions*. These people are seriously confused. Very roughly, religions require passionate communal displays of costly material commitments to gods, enabling mastery of existential anxieties under ritualised rhythmic sensory coordination in congregation and fellowship. (This characterisation is very rough because the costly material commitments may be to something other than gods: ancestor spirits, or means of escaping from non-natural regulative structures such as cycles of rebirth, and so forth.) Atheism and agnosticism do not require passionate communal displays, or costly material commitments to gods, or ritualised rhythmic sensory coordination in congregation and fellowship, or mastery of existential anxieties by the combination of these things. It is much closer to the mark to say that atheism and agnosticism are rejections of religion. Of course, this is not to say that atheists and agnostics have nothing in common with religious adherents. We are all human beings. We all have a range of existential anxieties. We all form beliefs on the basis of meagre information. We all learn most of what we know from other people. And so on. However, there is nothing in what we have in common that justifies the claim that atheism and agnosticism are religions.

Some people say that atheists and agnostics are *fundamentalists*. This claim, too, is seriously confused. In the intended sense, fundamentalism requires: (a) taking specific writings, teachings, and ideologies to be true under strictly literal interpretation; and (b) conservative insistence on the maintenance of ingroup/outgroup distinctions that is grounded in (a). There is nothing in atheism or agnosticism that requires any kind of ingroup identification; most atheists and agnostics are not affiliated with any atheistic or agnostic organisations or groups. Moreover, there is nothing in atheism or agnosticism that requires taking specific writings, teachings, and ideologies to be true under strictly literal interpretation in circumstances where others might prefer to see some other kind of interpretation of those writings, teachings, and ideologies. Of course, it is true that atheists claim that there are no gods, and that agnostics claim to suspend judgement on the question whether there are gods. But, equally, theists claim that it is true that there are gods. It is no more – or less – objectionable to have the beliefs of one of these parties declared in public than it is to have the beliefs of the other parties declared in public.

Some people suppose that atheists and agnostics are communists or fascists. Yet again, this claim is seriously confused. Communism and fascism are political ideologies. Very roughly, *communism* is aimed at the establishment of a socioeconomic order in which there are no social classes, states, or currencies, and in which there is common ownership of the means of production. Very roughly, *fascism* is a form of radical nationalism premised on: (a) violent elimination of 'decadent elements'; (b) national reconstruction that reverses alleged decline, humiliation, and victimisation; and (c) valorisation of youth, masculinity, and dictatorial charismatic leaders. There is nothing in atheism or agnosticism that requires adoption of either of these extreme political ideologies. Perhaps it is worth noting that states that adopt these political ideologies have often gone in for passionate communal displays of costly material commitments to *political leaders*, enabling mastery of existential anxieties under ritualised rhythmic sensory coordination in congregation and fellowship. While this indicates structural similarity between these political ideologies and religion, it opens up the same objections that were raised against the suggestion that atheism and agnosticism are religions. Of course, unlike the case of religion, there is no inconsistency between atheism or agnosticism and these political ideologies. Indeed, some communist and fascist states have been atheistic. But, outside of established communist regimes, most atheists are not communists.

Some people say that atheists and agnostics *hate* God. This is bizarre. Since atheists believe that there are no gods – and agnostics suspend judgement on the question whether there are gods – these people must mean to say that atheists and agnostics hate gods. Moreover, since the verdict of these people is based solely on the consideration that atheists and agnostics fail to believe that God exists, these people must mean to say that, for anything at all, if a person denies the existence of the thing, then the person hates the thing. So, by their own lights, these people most likely hate Santa Claus, Pegasus, Sherlock Holmes, Vulcan, perpetual motion machines, golden mountains, and miraculous cures for cancer. Given that they believe that none of these things exist, that seems a rather pointless waste of animosity.

1.11 Meaning

Some people say that talk about gods is meaningless. Some people – e.g. Ayer (1936:153) – say that this view is opposed to both atheism and agnosticism.

I think that it is impossible to take seriously the view that talk about gods is meaningless. Suppose you say: *it is meaningless to say that there are gods.* Is what you say meaningful? It must be that in order for 'it is meaningless to say that there are gods' to be meaningful, 'there are gods' is meaningful. But if 'there are gods' is meaningful, then 'it is meaningless to say that there are gods' is false. So the claim that *it is meaningless to say that there are gods* is self-defeating: if *it* is meaningful, then *it* is false; and, if *it* isn't meaningful, then *it* cannot be used to characterise your position.

The problem here is not merely one of characterisation. There are many claims that we are all inclined to accept would be meaningless if it is meaningless to say that there are gods. Consider, for example: many people believe that there are gods; many people deny that there are gods; many people suppose that, if there are gods, then those gods do not belong to the Norse pantheon; and so on. There seem to be very good reasons not to accept that talk about gods is meaningless.

But suppose that it were. Suppose that talk about gods is meaningless. Consider the claim that there are gods. Why shouldn't we just say that it is false that there are gods? If talk about gods is meaningless, then surely there are no gods? But, if that's right, then we can just assimilate the claim that talk about gods is meaningless into atheism: one way of being an atheist is to suppose that talk about gods is meaningless.

What if you suspend judgement on the question whether talk about gods is meaningless? In that case, it seems that you would also suspend judgement on the question whether there are gods. So - plausibly enough - one way of being an agnostic is to suspend judgement on the question whether talk about gods is meaningless.

Some people have proposed the introduction of new terms - *ignosticism* and *igtheism* - for positions that fall somewhere in the ballpark of the claim that talk about gods is meaningless. Somewhat ironically, it is doubtful that any clear and coherent meaning has been given to either of these terms, unless they are taken simply to be names for the view that talk about gods is meaningless. But, as we have just seen, if that is what these terms mean, then there is no need for them.

1.12   Further Distinctions?

Many authors have distinguished between different *kinds of atheism* and different *kinds of agnosticism*. Some authors distinguish between *strong* - hard, positive - *atheism* and *weak* - soft, negative - *atheism*. Some authors distinguish between *strong* - hard, closed, strict, permanent - *agnosticism* and *weak* - soft, open, flexible, impermanent - *agnosticism*.

In the case of atheism, the most common way to make out the distinction is to claim that, while strong atheists believe that there are no gods, weak atheists merely do not believe that there is at least one god. However, since agnostics and innocents also do not believe that there are gods, this way of making out the distinction counts agnosticism and innocence as types of atheism.

We have already seen that atheists can differ in (a) their degree of conviction that there are no gods; (b) the robustness of their conviction that there are no gods; (c) the degree of their desire that there be no gods; (d) the robustness of their desire that there be no gods; (e) their degree of interest in the question whether there are gods; (f) the robustness of their interest in the question whether there are gods; (g) their attitudes towards those who do not believe that there are no gods; (h) their attitude towards the epistemic status of their belief that there are no gods; and (i) their attitudes towards the claim that it is meaningless to say that there are no gods. While, in a particular context, it might be useful to use 'strong' and 'weak' to mark some salient distinction from this list – or in connection with other features that might be added to this list – it is clear that no useful purpose is served by further stipulation of a context-independent distinction between strong atheism and weak atheism.

In the case of agnosticism, there are various ways in which a distinction has been drawn. For some, strong agnosticism claims that agnosticism is rationally mandatory, while weak agnosticism claims that agnosticism is merely rationally permissible. For others, strong agnosticism claims that we cannot know whether there are gods, while weak agnosticism claims merely that we do not know whether there are gods. However, given that, as in the case of atheism, there is an open-ended list of features that could, according to context, support a distinction between strong agnosticism and weak agnosticism, no useful purpose is served by further stipulation of a context-independent distinction that makes use of these terms.

The fourfold distinction between atheists, agnostics, innocents, and theists is recommended on various grounds.

First, at least in principle, there is no overlap between the four categories. True enough, there may be borderline cases where it is unclear to which category someone belongs. But there cannot be someone who clearly belongs to more than one of these categories.

Second, at least in principle, there are no cases that fail to fit any of these categories. If someone is a borderline case, then they clearly belong to the 'disjunctive category' formed from the categories on whose borders they lie.

Third, the principles that determine who belongs to which category are simple, transparent, and uniform across the categories. How one is classified depends entirely upon the doxastic attitude that one takes towards the claim that there are no gods.

Fourth, the fourfold distinction fits well enough with ordinary use of these terms. As we have noted, there is divergent use of 'theist', 'atheist', and 'agnostic'. But it is implausible to suppose that there is a different regimentation of these terms that would both (a) give a satisfactory theoretical basis for that use, and (b) give a better fit with the full sweep of ordinary use.

1.13   Some Test Cases

Here are some things that people have said about atheism and agnosticism. You may find it useful to think about what the fourfold distinction – and the rest of the preceding discussion – entails for these claims. (I have included further prompts in parentheses. You might prefer to ignore these on first reading.)

1. 'All children are atheists, they have no idea of God.' (Baron d'Holbach, The System of Nature, 1770.) (Is someone who has no idea of God an atheist?)
2. 'I'm probably 20 percent atheist and 80 percent agnostic. I don't think anyone really knows.' (Brad Pitt, *Bild.com*, 2009) (Is there a position intermediate between atheism and agnosticism?)
3. 'The atheist is one who denies the assumptions of theism. He doesn't believe in a God because he has no reason for believing in a God. That's atheism.' (E. Haldeman-Julius *The Meaning of Atheism*, 1931) (Is supposing that one has no reason to believe in gods sufficient to make one an atheist?)
4. 'I contend that we are both atheists. I just believe in one fewer god than you do. When you understand why you dismiss all the other possible gods, you will understand why I dismiss yours.' (Stephen Roberts, tagline, 1995) (Do atheists dismiss all gods on the same grounds? Might atheists dismiss some particular gods on grounds specific to those particular gods?)
5. 'You don't have to be brave, or a saint, or a martyr, or even very smart to be an atheist. All you have to be able to say is "I don't know".' (Penn Jillette, *God, No!*, 2012) (Is this really enough?)

6. 'She believed in nothing. Only her scepticism kept her from being an atheist.' (Sartre, *The Words*, 1964) (Could there be someone who had no beliefs at all? Is it right to think that sceptics are those who have no beliefs?)

7. 'Agnostics are just atheists without balls.' (Stephen Colbert, *I am America*, 2007) (Would it be any worse to say that agnostics are just *theists* without balls?)

8. 'I did not marry the first girl that I fell in love with, because there was a tremendous religious conflict at that time. She was an atheist and I was an agnostic.' (Woody Allen, *NYU*, 1964) (Maybe we should just smile and move on. But perhaps it is worth asking: what makes this funny?)

9. 'Calling atheism a religion is like calling bald a hair colour' (Don Hirschberg, *Six Reasons Why*, 2008) (Is it utterly egregious to suppose that atheism is a religion?)

10. 'To count oneself as an atheist one need not claim to have a proof that no gods exist. One need merely think that the evidence on the god question is in about the same state as the evidence on the werewolf question.' (John McCarthy, webpage, 2013) (Must atheists suppose that it is about as likely that there are werewolves as it is that there are gods?)

1.14   Concluding Observations

I have argued that we should characterise atheists and agnostics in terms of their doxastic attitudes towards the claim that there are no gods: atheists believe that there are no gods, agnostics suspend judgement whether there are no gods.

I have also argued that not much follows from these characterisations. Merely being an atheist or an agnostic commits one to very little. There are many different substantive positions that entail commitment to atheism or agnosticism; it is these different substantive positions that are of primary interest in further discussion of the merits of atheism and agnosticism.

To learn more about the history of atheism and agnosticism, see Berman (1988), Blom (2010), Budd (1977), Curran (2012), Flynn (2007), Hunter and Wootton (1992), Jacoby (2013), Sheard (2014), Thrower (2000), and Whitmarsh (2015). For more about perceptions of atheism and agnosticism, see Gervais et al. (2011), Paul (2005), and Zuckerman (2009). For competing perspectives on the definition of 'atheism' and 'agnosticism', see Bullivant (2013), Draper (2017), and Gervais and Najile (2017).

2 Theoretical Background to Assessment

Given that we are clear about what atheism, agnosticism, and theism are, the biggest question to which we would like to have an answer is: which one of them should we adopt? That is a very large question, and not one that I am going to try to answer in this Element. Rather, I propose to do two things. First, in the present part of the Element, I shall sketch a framework within which discussion of the comparative merits of atheism, agnosticism, and theism can be addressed. Second, in the remaining parts of the Element, I shall try to say something about why you *might* find atheism or agnosticism attractive.

The discussion of the theoretical background to assessment is a harder slog than the introductory characterisation of atheism, agnosticism, and theism. Be prepared to take it slowly.

2.1 *Big Pictures*

What makes someone an atheist is their belief that there are no gods; what makes someone an agnostic is their suspension of judgement on the question whether there are gods. Atheism is characterised by the claim that there are no gods; agnosticism is characterised by its commitment to nothing more than the claim that either it is the case that there are no gods or it is the case that there is at least one god. Atheistic big pictures – worldviews, theories of everything – include or entail the claim that there are no gods; agnostic big pictures include the claim that either it is the case that there are no gods or it is the case that there is at least one god but include or entail *neither* the claim that there are no gods *nor* the claim that there is at least one god.

Particular atheists and agnostics may not have very well-developed big pictures. Even the most intelligent, thoughtful, reflective, well-informed atheists and agnostics have big pictures that are susceptible of improvement in ever so many ways. Commitment to atheism or agnosticism does not prevent atheists and agnostics from revising their big pictures in countless different ways. An ongoing commitment to atheism is nothing more than a commitment to the claim that the *best* big pictures are atheistic big pictures; an ongoing commitment to agnosticism is nothing more than a commitment to the claim that the *best* big pictures are agnostic big pictures.

Given that our big pictures are radically incomplete, it might seem puzzling that we can form views about the comparative merits of best big pictures. Given that there is so much that we do not know – even collectively – how can anyone be justified in claiming that one kind of best big picture is better than other kinds of best big pictures?

Consider a simple case, e.g. the claim that Canberra is the capital of Australia. Why should we be confident that all best big pictures that involve consideration of this claim will accept it? Because (a) we have overwhelming reason to accept the claim now, and (b) we have overwhelming reason to think that there is nothing that we are not yet aware of that is going to defeat this claim. A crucial part of the overwhelming reason to accept the claim now is the universal expert consensus – in encyclopaedias and reliable works of reference – that Canberra is the capital of Australia. And a crucial part of the overwhelming reason to think that there is nothing that we are not yet aware of that is going to defeat this claim is that same universal expert consensus – in encyclopaedias and reliable works of reference – that Canberra is the capital of Australia. How could it turn out that Canberra is not the capital of Australia, given that there is universal expert consensus that Canberra is the capital of Australia? What could *explain* the universal expert consensus – e.g. in encyclopaedias and reliable works of reference – that

Canberra is the capital of Australia if it is not the case that Canberra is the capital of Australia?

In general, justification for the claim that one *kind* of best big picture is better than other kinds of best big pictures turns on two considerations: first, that the claims that characterise the favoured kind of best big picture are the best claims to make on the basis of everything of which we are currently aware; and, second, that we have no reason to suppose that there are further considerations of which we are not currently aware that will make a difference to the evaluation of those claims. So long as we are confident that (a) we have *all* of the relevant considerations in view, and (b) we have appraised those considerations correctly, we can be confident in our judgement about what best big pictures will say or entail concerning the matter at hand.

2.2   Method

In order to satisfy ourselves that our big pictures are the best big pictures, we need a method for comparing big pictures. In the case in which we are currently interested, we would like to use the method to compare best atheistic big pictures, best agnostic big pictures, and best theistic big pictures.

In principle, the method is straightforward. First, we *articulate* the various big pictures: we write them out in exhaustive detail. Second, we provide an *internal review* of each big picture, looking for inconsistencies; where big pictures are inconsistent, we can safely set them aside. Third, we *compare the virtues* of those big pictures that survive internal review: more virtuous big pictures are better than less virtuous big pictures.

In practice, we cannot follow this method.

In practice, we cannot articulate our big pictures in exhaustive detail. At best, we make judgements about what is relevant to the assessment of given big pictures and then articulate all of those big pictures, to the same level of detail with the same level of care and attention, in connection with all relevant matters.

In practice, checking for inconsistency is an endless task: except in special cases, it is very hard to establish consistency; except in special cases, it is an open question whether articulated big pictures are consistent. At best, we use current results as a defeasible guide: if it has not been shown that given big pictures are inconsistent, then we take it as a working hypothesis that those big pictures are consistent.

In practice, weighing virtues of big pictures is enormously controversial. In the case in which we are interested – weighing the virtues of best atheistic big pictures, best agnostic big pictures, and best theistic big pictures – there is a very large range of relevant considerations, and a wide range of methods that have been proposed for weighing them.

2.3 Data

When we weigh the virtues of competing big pictures, one of the primary considerations is how well the competing big pictures explain *data*. What is data? Given our account of big pictures, the most plausible thing to say is that data is everything that is not in dispute between the competing big pictures. For any claim at all, if that claim is in common between the competing big pictures, then that claim is data. And, for any claim at all, if that claim is not in common between the competing big pictures, then that claim is not data.

Suppose that, in the dispute in which we are interested, theists claim that (a) certain miraculous events have occurred, and (b) those events are to be explained as the outcomes of actions of the gods. If atheists deny that those events occurred – and agnostics suspend judgement on the question whether those events occurred – then it should not be taken to be a relative advantage of theism that it affords an explanation of the occurrence of those events; rather, the occurrence of those events is just part of what is in dispute between these atheists, agnostics, and theists. Of course, there is something here on which atheists, agnostics, and theists all agree – namely, that there are *reports* of the occurrence of these *and other* miraculous events – and this *is* data whose explanation does count in the comparative assessment of atheism, agnosticism, and theism.

Suppose that, in the dispute in which we are interested, atheists claim that (a) there has been several hundred million years of animal suffering, and (b) that this suffering is best explained as the outworking of natural selection. If theists deny that there has been several hundred million years of animal suffering – or if agnostics suspend judgement on the question whether there has been several hundred million years of animal suffering – then it should not be taken to be a relative advantage of atheism that it affords an explanation of that animal suffering; rather, the occurrence of that animal suffering is part of what is in dispute between atheists, agnostics, and theists. Of course, there is much here on which atheists, agnostics, and theists agree – e.g. that the expert members of national science academies unanimously maintain that there has been several hundred million years of animal suffering – and this *is* data whose explanation does count in the comparative assessment of atheism, agnosticism, and theism.

It should not be supposed that everything that I am calling 'data' will have an explanation in at least some best big pictures: it may be that there are some claims which are primitive in all best big pictures. The essential feature of data is not that, in some big pictures, it actually has an explanation that must be figured into calculations of comparative theoretical virtue; rather, the essential feature of data is that it is a potential target in big pictures for explanations that would figure in calculations of comparative big picture virtue.

2.4 Virtues

There are various different kinds of virtues of scientific theories: (1) *internal virtues*: e.g. consistency of theory and consistency with data; (2) *utility*: e.g. fruitfulness, applicability, and predictive power; (3) *minimisation of theoretical commitments*: e.g. simplicity, beauty, and unity; and (4) *maximisation of explanatory breadth and depth*: e.g. width of cosmological role and fit with well-established science.

In our assessment of big pictures, we give separate treatment to the internal virtues, and we take no account of utility (since, for example, big pictures do not generate testable predictions). So, as many people have recognised, when we assess big pictures, we are essentially interested in a trade-off between minimisation of theoretical commitments and maximisation of explanatory breadth and depth. The best big pictures are those that make the best trade-off between minimisation of theoretical commitments and maximisation of explanatory breadth and depth.

In general, determining what is the best trade-off between minimisation of theoretical commitments and maximisation of explanatory breadth and depth is a difficult and controversial matter.

Bayesians suppose that we must cast the entire discussion in terms of probabilities: better theories are those that have comparatively higher probabilities of truth. Very crudely – and I mean very crudely – if T1 and T2 are competing theories, and E is our total relevant evidence, then (a) the prior probabilities Pr(T1) and Pr(T2) are inversely proportioned to the strength of the theoretical commitments of T1 and T2; (b) the likelihoods Pr(E/T1) and Pr(E/T2) are directly proportioned to the explanatory breadth and depth of T1 and T2 with respect to E; and – by the odds version of Bayes Theorem – (c) the ratio of the posterior probabilities Pr(T1/E) and Pr(T2/E) is determined by the relevant prior probabilities and likelihoods:

$$\frac{Pr(T1/E)}{Pr(T2/E)} = \frac{Pr(E/T1).Pr(T1)}{Pr(E/T2).Pr(T2)}$$

In other words: the more that theories postulate, the lower their prior probabilities; the more that theories explain, the higher their likelihoods; but the more that theories postulate, the more they can explain. And the higher the posterior probability, the better the theory, given the evidence.

While in general you need numbers in order to be able to do Bayesian calculations, there are special cases. If you can show that one theory has fewer commitments than a second theory, but nowhere fares worse with respect to explanatory breadth and depth than that second theory, then you can immediately conclude that the first theory is more virtuous than the second theory. We can illustrate this idea with a simple example.

Suppose that someone is puzzled by the fact that the earth doesn't seem to be falling through space and postulates that the earth doesn't fall because it is supported by a giant elephant. When we compare the elephant theory to the no-elephant theory, it may seem that the elephant theory has an explanatory advantage: it explains why the earth isn't falling. True, this explanation comes at the cost of postulating a new entity – the giant elephant – but, according to the proponent of the elephant theory, the cost is worth paying.

The analysis that we have just given is wrong. In the no-elephant theory, the earth just hangs in space. It is a primitive – unexplained – commitment of that theory that the earth is a 'hanger'. In the elephant theory, the elephant just hangs in space – the elephant is a 'hanger'. Each theory has one 'hanger': in point of commitment to 'hangers', there is no difference between the theories. So, clearly, the postulation of the elephant is purely gratuitous: it makes no reduction in the number of 'hangers' – even though the only thing that it is designed to do is to make it the case that the earth is not a 'hanger' – and yet it introduces additional theoretical cost.

Note, too, that it won't help to postulate that the elephant is an 'intrinsic hanger': i.e. that it is just in the nature of the giant elephant to 'hang'. For, if it is acceptable to postulate that the elephant is an 'intrinsic hanger', then it is equally appropriate to postulate that the earth is an 'intrinsic hanger' – i.e., that it is just in the nature of the earth to 'hang'. Once we update the no-elephant theory appropriately, the postulation of the elephant remains purely gratuitous.

The view that the earth just hangs in space is more virtuous than the view that the earth rests on the back of a giant elephant that just hangs in space: it is more theoretically economical, and – when the accounting is done properly – the elephant theory has no greater explanatory virtue than the no-elephant theory.

In the forthcoming discussion, we shall neither assume that we *can* supply the numbers that are needed for Bayesian calculations nor assume that we *cannot* supply the numbers that are needed for Bayesian calculations. We will not, ourselves, be making any numerical Bayesian calculations.

2.5 Derivations

Demonstrating inconsistency requires derivation. In order to show that a set of claims is inconsistent, we list the claims, and then add new claims to our list that follow, as a matter of logic, from claims already on our list; eventually, we arrive at an explicit contradiction, i.e. a claim of the form *C and not-C*. More generally, in order to show that a given claim is a logical consequence of some further claims, we list the further claims, and then add new claims to our list that follow, as a matter of logic, from claims already on our list; eventually, we add the given claim to our list.

A fundamental result of classical logic tells us that, if a set of claims are jointly inconsistent, then the negation of any one of those claims can be derived from all the rest. If A, B, and C are jointly inconsistent, then we can derive not-C from A and B, and we can derive not-B from A and C, and we can derive not-A from B and C. So, we can derive an inconsistency from a set of claims that includes the claim that *there is at least one god* exactly when we can derive the claim that *there are no gods* from the remaining claims in the set. And, we can derive an inconsistency from a set of claims that includes the claim that *there are no gods* exactly when we can derive the claim that *there is at least one god* from the remaining claims in the set.

In the second – internal – stage of the evaluation of competing big pictures, we check to see whether we can derive a contradiction from claims that belong to those big pictures. We will be able to do this for a given big picture exactly when we can derive the negation of the claim that chacterises a given big picture from other claims all of which belong to that big picture.

Obviously enough, we can derive contradictions by putting together claims from competing big pictures. The simplest way to see this is to consider putting together the characterising claims of competing big pictures. As we noted way back, 'there is at least one god' and 'there are no gods' are contradictories; they cannot both be true. But, quite generally, deriving contradictions by putting together claims from competing big pictures tells us nothing about which big picture to prefer: such derivations can play no role in deciding which is the better big picture.

An important consequence of this last observation is that one cannot use existing 'proofs' of the existence or non-existence of gods to decide between competing big pictures *unless* all of the premises belong to the big picture that is being targeted by the 'proof'. A fully adequate response to any 'proof' of the falsity of the characterising claim of your big picture is the observation that your big picture neither contains nor entails one of the premises of that 'proof'.

We do not currently have any derivations that show that best atheistic big pictures are inconsistent, nor do we currently have any derivations that show that best theistic big pictures are inconsistent. Consequently, we do not currently have any successful derivations of the claim that there are no gods, nor do we currently have any successful derivations of the claim that there is at least one god. While it cannot be ruled out that we might come to have successful derivations of one of these claims in the future, I think that track record – in combination with careful examination of extant derivations – should lead us to suppose that it is extraordinarily unlikely that we shall ever have successful derivations of these claims. In order to make progress in the evaluation of atheistic, agnostic, and theistic big pictures, there is no option but to move on to the third stage of comparative evaluation: we need to consider whether we can show that one type of best big picture has greater theoretical virtue than the other types of best big picture.

Perhaps it will help to consider a concrete example. Suppose that, somehow, it is determined that the best view to take about God is that, if it is possible that God exists, then it is necessary that God exists. Given this assumption, best theistic big pictures that suppose that God exists will be committed to all of the following three claims: it is possible that God exists; God exists; and it is necessary that God exists. Moreover, given this same assumption, best atheistic big pictures will be committed to all of the following three claims: it is possible that God does not exist; God does not exist; and it is necessary that God does not exist.

Consider the following standard modal ontological argument:

1. If it is possible that God exists, then it is necessary that God exists. (Premise)
2. It is possible that God exists. (Premise)
3. (Therefore) God exists. (From 1 and 2.)

This argument is clearly valid, i.e. the conclusion is obviously a logical consequence of the two premises. But, while the relevant best theistic big pictures include 2 and 3, the relevant best atheistic big pictures include neither 2 nor 3. This argument gives no support to the relevant best theistic big pictures over best atheistic big pictures, just as the argument:

1. If it is possible that God exists, then it is necessary that God exists. (Premise)
2. It is possible that God does not exist. (Premise)
3. (Therefore) God does not exist. (From 1 and 2.)

gives no support to the relevant best atheistic big pictures over best theistic big pictures. (Although it may not be immediately obvious, this argument is also valid. Given that it is possible that God does not exist, it is not necessary that God exists. But, from 1, if it is not necessary that God exists, then it is not possible that God exists. And if it is not possible that God exists, then God does not exist.)

For more about Bayesian theory choice, see Earman (1996), Horwich (1982), Swinburne (2002), and Talbott (2008). For introductions to logic, see Forbes (1994), Priest (2000), and Shapiro

(2013). For further discussion of modal ontological arguments, see van Inwagen (2018) and Rowe (1976).

3   A Case for Preferring Atheism to Theism

One common objection to atheism is that it cannot be rational to maintain that there are no gods. What reason could you have for thinking that there are no gods? Why couldn't it be that – by luck or design – you either don't have what it takes to recognise that there are gods or you have missed out on acquiring the reasons that other people have for thinking that there are gods?

Sometimes we do have reason for thinking that there is nothing of a certain kind. Is there a carton of milk in the fridge? All you need to do is open the fridge to look. If you cannot see a carton of milk in the fridge, and if there is nothing in the fridge that a carton of milk might be hidden behind, they you are justified in forming the belief that there is no carton of milk in the fridge.

If you have any doubt whether there might be a carton of milk in the fridge, you can ask one or more other people to look. So long as no one has any malicious intent, and so long as those you ask have adequate functioning powers of perception and reason, everyone else who looks will return the same verdict that you do. Of course, there is nothing special about cartons of milk: for an enormous range of 'everyday objects' in 'everyday circumstances', there is uniform agreement, among those with adequate powers of perception and reason, about the existence and location of these kinds of things. Moreover, in the case of cartons of milk – as in the case of other 'everyday objects' – it would be just plain silly to suppose that there are invisible, ineffable cartons of milk whose existence is disclosed only to a privileged subset of those who look for them. Once we have checked properly, if we have not found a carton of milk in the fridge, the proper conclusion to be drawn is that there are no cartons of milk in the fridge, not even invisible, ineffable ones.

Perhaps you might think that, since it would just be plain silly to believe in invisible, ineffable milk cartons, this case has no relevance for the question of the rationality of the belief that there are no gods. But consider, instead, the case of fairies. Belief in fairies has been widespread. Famously, in the 1920s, Sir Arthur Conan Doyle (the author of the Sherlock Holmes stories) defended the existence of the Cottingley fairies (see Doyle (1922/2006), Griffiths and Lynch (2009), and Losure (2012)).

While fairies are typically considered to be small, the most often cited reasons why most of us fail to encounter them is that they are both shy and intuitive: they do not like to be seen, and they are very good at noticing that someone might be about to observe them. While they will, on occasion, reveal themselves, almost always they do so only to those who are not likely to be widely regarded as credible witnesses – e.g. 'pure' young children.

Most rational, educated adults believe that there are no fairies. It is not merely that most rational, educated adults suspend judgement on the questions whether, say, they have fairies at the bottom of their gardens. And it is not merely that most rational, educated adults suspend judgement on the question whether there are *shy, intuitive* fairies at the bottom of their gardens, i.e. fairies of a kind that they would not detect even if they looked for them. Just as you can rationally believe that there are no milk cartons in your fridge, so, too, you can rationally believe that there are no fairies at the bottom of your garden. And it is not merely that most rational educated adults rationally believe that there are no fairies at the bottom of their gardens – most rational educated adults also rationally believe that *there are no fairies anywhere at all.*

Atheists think that what goes for fairies also goes for gods: they think that they have good enough reasons to believe that there are no gods. While the details of atheists' cases against gods are different from the details of cases against fairies, the outcome is the same: atheists take themselves not to have any first-order reasons to believe that there are gods, and they take it that the second-order reasons that they have are not strong enough even to give them reason to suspend judgement on the question.

In what follows, I shall set out one kind of case for atheism. It is not a case that all atheists will accept. However, it serves to illustrate the kind of case that atheists might give.

3.1 Outline

The case to be set out here is, in the first instance, a case for naturalism – i.e., a case for the claim that the best big pictures are big pictures that maintain or entail that (a) there are none but natural causal entities with none but natural causal properties, and (b) well-established science is the touchstone for identifying causal entities and causal powers.

The case has two main parts. First, it is argued that best naturalist big pictures are minimal among best big pictures: there is nothing to which best naturalist big pictures are committed to which other best big pictures are not also committed. Second, it is argued that best naturalist big pictures are maximal among best big pictures: there is nothing that is explained better by other best big pictures than by best naturalist big pictures.

Given that best theistic big pictures have additional commitments – in particular, commitments to gods – that best naturalistic big pictures do not have, and given that best theistic big pictures do not anywhere give better explanations than best naturalistic big pictures, best theistic big pictures are inferior to best naturalistic big pictures. But that's just to say that some best big pictures that maintain or entail that there are no gods are better than all best big pictures that maintain or entail that there are gods. Which is just to say that we should believe that there are no gods.

3.2 Minimality

The case that best naturalistic big pictures are minimal in the class of best big pictures is relatively straightforward.

Every best big picture is committed to the causal entities and causal powers that are postulated by or taken for granted in

well-established science. Every best big picture is committed to
electrons, atoms, molecules, proteins, viruses, organelles, cells,
plants, animals, cookware, books, houses, cars, roads, cities,
power grids, currencies, oceans, planets, solar systems, stars,
galaxies, and so forth. And every big picture is committed to the
causal powers of all of these things: attraction, repulsion, expan-
sion, radiation, ingestion, digestion, infection, locomotion, ero-
sion, and so on. But, among best big pictures, naturalistic big
pictures are unique in being committed to *only* these things.
Other best big pictures are committed to further causal entities
and causal powers: e.g. fairies and the non-natural powers of
fairies, or gods and the non-natural powers of gods.

Some might think that we should here be considering only
fundamental commitments: commitments to those fundamental
entities and fundamental powers from which all other entities and
powers are composed. Naturalists need not disagree. If there is
some collection of fundamental natural entities and fundamental
natural powers from which all other natural entities and natural
powers are composed, then best naturalistic big pictures will
recognise this, and, in the proposed sense, best naturalistic big
pictures will be committed to just those fundamental natural entities and fundamental natural powers. Since fairies and gods do not
number among either the fundamental or the non-fundamental
natural entities, and since at least some of the powers of fairies and
gods do not number among either the fundamental or the non-
fundamental natural powers, accommodation of this point does
nothing to undermine the claim that the commitments of best
naturalistic big pictures are minimal in the class of best big
pictures.

Some might think that there are alternative metaphysical stand-
points from which naturalism can be seen to be more than minimal. Consider, for example, the Berkeleyan idealist view according
to which natural objects and natural powers are ideas in the mind
of God. Don't Berkeleyan idealists have fewer commitments than
naturalists? Not at all! For each (fundamental) natural entity, the
Berkeleyan idealist is committed to a distinct corresponding idea

in the mind of God. For each (fundamental) natural power, the Berkeleyan idealist is committed to a distinct corresponding idea in the mind of God. In terms of fundamental commitments, there is parity – except that the Berkeleyan idealist is also committed to God (and perhaps to more besides). When we make a proper accounting, the (fundamental) commitments of Berkeleyan idealists exceed the (fundamental) commitments of naturalists. (Might a different kind of theist say that, since there is just one idea in the mind of God – the idea of everything that there is – theism has fewer commitments than naturalism? Not at all! Naturalists can, with no less justice, say that there is just one thing: natural reality. Whatever dissatisfaction attends to this naturalist claim attends with equal measure to the corresponding theistic claim.)

Monotheists who think that God created the natural world ex nihilo are particularly poorly placed to dispute the claim that best naturalistic big pictures are more minimal than best monotheistic big pictures. It seems obvious that those who suppose that causal reality is exhausted by natural reality have a more minimal view than those who suppose that, *in addition*, causal reality contains something that is the cause of the existence of natural reality. But, if what has been argued in this section is correct, it is not just best monotheistic big pictures that have more commitments than best naturalistic big pictures; all other best big pictures have more commitments than best naturalistic big pictures.

3.3 Maximality

The case that the best naturalistic big pictures are maximal in the class of best big pictures is complicated, and susceptible of more or less unlimited addition to its details. For reasons that will soon be apparent – if they are not apparent already – any filling out of this case is, in a certain sense, incomplete.

In what follows, I shall divide domains, concerning which it might be wondered whether explanations in best naturalistic big pictures are bettered by explanations in best theistic big pictures, into two major kinds: 'first-order' domains and 'second-order' domains. Roughly, 'second-order' domains concern the testimony of human individuals and groups, while 'first-order' domains are concerned with something other than the testimony of human individuals and groups.

The 'first-order' domains that I shall consider concern: (1) general causal features of reality; (2) general 'design' features of reality; and (3) 'mental' features of reality. The 'second-order' domains that I shall consider concern: (1) reports of 'anomalous' phenomena; (2) reports of religious 'experience'; (3) reports of 'holy books'; and (4) reports of divine 'communication'. For each of these domains, I shall set out an argument that the explanation provided by best naturalistic big pictures for data in the given domain is no worse that the explanation provided by best theistic big pictures for that data.

Since there is a lot to get through, and since we are merely providing sketches of arguments that can be developed in much greater detail, we shall move fairly quickly.

3.4 Causation

Some people think that theism can have an explanatory advantage when it comes to the existence of natural causal reality: unlike their naturalistic counterparts, theists can have an explanation of the existence of natural causal reality that appeals to the creative activities of gods.

These people are mistaken, for much the same reason that elephant theorists are mistaken in thinking that the elephant theory has an explanatory advantage over the no-elephant theory (see Section 2.4).

Consider causal reality. The existence of causal reality cannot have a causal explanation. Causes are distinct from their effects; consequently, causes of the existence of causal reality both would and would not be parts of causal reality. So, if there is an explanation of the existence of causal reality, it is a non-causal explanation. What property could causal reality have that would explain its existence? There is only one plausible candidate: causal reality exists of necessity; it could not have failed to be the case that causal reality exists. But, if we do best to suppose that we can appeal to necessity to explain the existence of causal reality, then best naturalistic big pictures will include the claim that natural reality exists of necessity. And, if best theistic big pictures include or entail the claim that there are gods that exist of necessity and that create natural reality, while best naturalistic big pictures include or entail the claim that natural reality exists of necessity, then there is no difference in the ultimate explanation of the existence of causal reality on these two types of best big pictures. Ultimately, however you slice the pie, the existence of causal reality turns out to be a matter of primitive, unexplained necessity.

Of course, at least for all that we have argued, it could turn out that the best big pictures tell some other story about the existence of causal reality. Perhaps it is a matter of brute contingency. Perhaps it is a matter of infinite regress. But, whatever the story is, best naturalistic big pictures and best theistic big pictures will incorporate it in ways that entail that there is no explanatory advantage that accrues to either.

3.5 Design

Some people think that theism can have an explanatory advantage when it comes to the 'fine-tuning' of natural reality: unlike their naturalistic counterparts, theists can have an explanation of the 'fine-tuning' of natural causal reality that appeals to the creative activities of gods.

In the current standard model of particle physics, there are freely adjustable parameters for which the following is true: had a given freely adjustable parameter taken a value only very slightly different from its actual value – with all else being fixed – then either our universe would have been very short-lived, or else it would have exploded so rapidly that it would always have consisted of more or less nothing but empty space. Either way, our universe would not have contained the familiar causal objects that it contains: electrons, atoms, molecules, proteins, viruses, organelles, cells, plants, animals, cookware, books, houses, cars, roads, cities, power grids, currencies, oceans, planets, solar systems, stars, galaxies, and so forth. In the parlance adopted by many participants in this discussion, it seems that our universe is 'fine-tuned' for the existence of these familiar causal objects.

To give theists the strongest position, I shall suppose – for the purposes of this discussion – that natural causal reality is not part of a multiverse or ensemble of universes. Even so, it is a mistake to suppose that theists have an explanatory advantage when it comes to the 'fine-tuning' of our universe.

We are to suppose that at some point in causal reality, the values of the adjustable parameters are set: they take on values that, absent intervention, they will continue to have; and we are also to suppose that there is no subsequent intervention.

There are two possibilities: either the point at which the values are set is the initial point of causal reality, or the point at which the values are set is a non-initial point of causal reality.

If the point at which the values are set is the initial point of causal reality, then there cannot be anything that assigns those values at that point, because any such assigning would be a causal transition that is prior to all of causal reality. So, if the point at which the values are set is the initial point of causal reality, then, if there is an explanation of the taking on of those values, it can only be that the taking on of those values is necessary. Whether or not there is an explanation of the taking on of those values, there is no explanatory advantage that accrues to theism or to naturalism: best naturalistic big pictures say that, at the initial point of natural causal reality, the parameters take their current values; best theistic big pictures say that, at the initial point of causal reality, the gods' preferences for the values of the parameters are set to the current values. Either way, the ultimate explanation – if there is one – is the same: brute necessity.

If the point at which the values are set is a non-initial point of causal reality, then there is a transition from a state in which the values of the parameters have not been fixed to a state in which the values of the parameters are fixed. A transition of this kind must be chancy: in this case, it is a matter of brute contingency that the values that are taken on are the current values. For naturalism, at the transition point, the parameters take their current values; for theists, at the transition point, the gods' preferences for the parameters are fixed to the current values. Either way, in this case, there is no further explanation why these values rather than other values, and so no explanatory advantage that accrues to either side.

Putting it all together: no matter what is the best explanation of the 'fine-tuning' of our universe, there is no explanatory advantage here for best theistic big pictures over best naturalistic big pictures.

3.6 Mind

Some people think that theism can have an explanatory advantage over naturalism when it comes to the presence of mindedness – consciousness, reason, memory, perception, action, emotion, attitude, and the like – in causal reality.

Naturalists suppose that mindedness is *late and local*: the only minded entities that we currently know about are relatively recently evolved biological organisms on our planet. It is an open question whether there are relatively recently evolved biological organisms on other planets; and it is an open question whether there are – or will be – artificial minded entities that are downstream causal products of the activities of biological organisms. But that's it: there neither have been, nor are, nor will be any other kinds of minded entities in causal reality.

Naturalists also suppose that we need appeal to nothing more than biological processes in organisms, the local environments of those organisms, and the local social and biological evolutionary histories of those organisms, in order to explain the various aspects of their mindedness. For example, for minded entities to be conscious just is for them to be engaged in certain kinds of neural processing; and for minded entities to be perceiving their immediate environments just is for them, in those environments, to be engaged in certain kinds of neural processing that have been appropriately shaped by local, social, and evolutionary history and that are appropriately causally related to those environments.

The naturalist account of mindedness is minimal, both in the extent that it accords to mindedness, and in the resources that it invokes in explaining mindedness. Theists of one stripe or another add to this minimal account one or more of the following claims: (a) there are other minded entities: gods, angels, demons, and the like; (b) mindedness is ubiquitous: everything has proto-mental properties; (c) natural reality is minded; (d) particular mountains/trees/rocks/etc. are minded; (e) particular weapons/relics/utensils/etc. are minded; (f) there can be transfer of instances of mindedness between organisms; (g) there can be mindedness in the absence of organisms; (h) mindedness depends upon the existence of entities – minds – that are not located in our universe; (i) the only fundamental things are minds and their mindedness; and so on. But is there any data that is better explained by these kinds of claims than by naturalism?

Some say that these kinds of claims can explain how it is possible for there to be cosmic justice and life after death. But cosmic justice and life after death are not data: naturalists – among others – do not accept that there is either cosmic justice or life after death. So – at least pending further considerations – there is no explanatory advantage to be gained in appealing to them.

Some say that there is scientific evidence for cosmic justice and/or life after death in, for example, reports of near-death and out-of-body experiences. But no reputable scientific meta-analyses support claims about the veridicality of near-death and out-of-body experiences. Rather, meta-analyses support the claim that these experiences are comprehensively explained in terms of neural insult.

Some – e.g. Chalmers (1996) – hold that there could be creatures that share our neural states and processes but that lack key features of our mindedness, e.g. subjective conscious experience. Those who insist that subjective conscious experience just is engagement in certain kinds of neural processing deny that there could be any such creatures. So, it certainly is not data that there could be such creatures.

Some – e.g. Plantinga (2012) and Reppert (2009) – argue that our reasoning capacities could not be a socially moulded mix of evolutionary adaptations and exaptations. But those arguments assume the reliability of our reasoning capacities in domains in which it is obvious that our reasoning capacities are highly unreliable: philosophy, religion, politics, and the like. When we make a more accurate assessment of the reliability of our reasoning capacities, we see that that assessment supports the claim that our reasoning capacities are a socially moulded mix of evolutionary adaptations and exaptations.

While there is much more that could be said to fill out these brief remarks, it should be clear enough how naturalists arrive at the view that considerations about mindedness give no explanatory advantage to theists.

3.7 Anomaly

Some people think that theism can have an explanatory advantage when it comes to reports of the occurrence of miracles. Religions are replete with such reports, in their accounts of the lives and deeds of their founding figure, in the episodes recorded in their central texts, in the accounts passed down in their oral traditions, and, often enough, in their contemporary deliverances.

In order to assess this claim, we need to consider the wider background. True enough, if miracle reports were accurate, they would pose severe challenges to naturalists: miracle reports typically describe events that defy explanation by well-established science. But it should be remembered not only (a) that all religions have their own miracle reports, but also (b) that there is a vast range of other reports that are prima facie challenges to well-established science. Consider, for example, reports across the extraordinary range of conspiracy theories, alternative medicines, and cryptids (creatures recognised only in folklore, such as chupacabras, sasquatch and yeti) that are prima facie challenges to well-established science.

It is obvious to pretty much everyone that almost all of these reports of 'anomalous' entities and events are cut from the same cloth, and it is obvious to pretty much everyone that almost all of these reports are false. Moreover, it is obvious to pretty much everyone how these reports are to be explained. We are all fallible; we all make lots of errors. We all like to have tidy explanations; we are all disposed to make stuff up. We are all prone to false attributions of agency; we are all prone to seeing agency where there is only happenstance. Moreover, we are all disposed to believe what we are told by those we take to be authoritative, and we are all disposed to pass on things that we are told by those we take to be authoritative. It is entirely unsurprising that there is local uptake of falsehoods, including, in particular, minimally counterintuitive falsehoods, i.e. falsehoods concerning entities and events that are strikingly different from familiar entities and events along just one or two dimensions. Inevitably, some falsehoods become entrenched in particular communities; inevitably, some falsehoods become attractors for further theorisation; inevitably, some falsehoods receive institutional support. While it is never the case that these falsehoods are supported by well-established science, and while it is never the case that these falsehoods have global acceptance, these falsehoods can become deeply entrenched, and they can be accepted by large populations for millennia.

Naturalists suppose that something like the above account – which everyone accepts for some range of cases – applies to all cases. All reports of miracles and sightings of cryptids, and all conspiracy theories and alternative medicines, that constitute prima facie challenges to well-established science should be rejected. Given their provenance, it would be absurd to give significant credence to reports of any of these things. No one has the time to exhaustively trace the histories of all of the reports of these things, no one has the time to exhaustively weigh the relative merits of the cases that can be made for each of them, but it would be impermissibly arbitrary to accept some without having checked – with at least the same degree of sympathy and attention – whether there are better cases for others.

Given the entirely uniform account that naturalists give of the full range of reports of entities and events that are anomalous with respect to well-established science, it is highly implausible to claim that there is an explanatory disadvantage that accrues to them. When theists from different religions disagree about who really worked miracles, and about which texts accurately record miracles, and about which contemporary events really are miracles that support particular religions, it is clearly an explanatory advantage for naturalists to be able to chalk all of this disagreement up to special pleading.

3.8 Experience

Some people think that theism can have an explanatory advantage when it comes to reports of religious experience. Of course, there are many different kinds of religious experiences: some religious experience is directly generated by religious practice, some religious experience is merely facilitated response to what is acknowledged to be the natural world, some religious experience involves (alleged) witnessing of miracles, some religious experience involves dreams and visions, some religious experience involves mystical – sacred, spiritual – episodes. I shall consider only the last category of religious experiences here.

Mystical experience is of various kinds: *ecstatic* experiences of divine possession; *numinous* experiences of fear, compulsion, and personality; *unitive* experiences of evanescence, ineffability, passivity, pedagogical value, and tranquillity; *salvific* experiences (allegedly) accompanying liberation, enlightenment, and rebirth; and *natural* experiences of oneness with the natural world.

All of these kinds of mystical experiences are claimed to have negligible communicable content; it is not clear that they give any particular support to some religions above others. And it is hard to see any reason for thinking that these mystical experiences support theism over naturalism. Much mystical experience is generated by conditions that are correlated with poor performance on even quite simple cognitive tasks. Even when they are not generated by such conditions, there is no reason to suppose that these experiences have any significance for the choice between best theistic big pictures and best naturalistic big pictures. There are many experiences that we can find hard to interpret – feelings of being shadowed, cold shivers, unprovoked bursts of joy, racing thoughts, and so forth. All of these kinds of experiences can be expected to have explanations in terms of mature cognitive science and evolutionary theory. Certainly, it is no mark against naturalism that it is to be expected that best naturalistic big pictures will provide a uniform account of all the various kinds of hard-to-interpret experiences, including mystical experiences.

3.9 Scripture

Some people think that theism can have an explanatory advantage when it comes to the existence and content of the central texts of theistic religions.

Some people suppose that there is evidence for the non-natural origins of the central texts of given religions in (1) alleged literary merits of those texts, (2) successful detailed predictions of future events in those texts, and (3) confirmation of the material that is found in those texts in (a) the alleged superiority of the distinctive moral and social teachings in those texts, (b) the advanced scientific knowledge that is contained in those texts, and (c) the inclusion of information in those texts that could not possibly have been possessed by the authors of those texts.

These considerations are all very weak. (1) Most central religious texts are canonical literary works for adherents of those religions; judgements about the literary merits of those texts is hopelessly controversial. (2) Given what we know about the redaction of these texts – and the uncertainties involved in dating their initial composition and subsequent redaction – there is no consensus on even one successful detailed future prediction in any central religious text; (3) Given the many barriers to confident interpretation of these texts, the many uncertainties about their redaction and reproduction, and the depth of disagreement about moral and social matters, there is no consensus that any of the central religious texts is marked by any distinctive kind of superiority.

Some people have claimed that, because there is evidence in the historical record for the existence of natural entities and the occurrence of natural events that are recorded in those texts, we have evidence for the reliability of those who compiled them, and hence reason to accept the claims that they make about the existence of non-natural entities and the occurrence of non-natural events.

This argument is also very weak. Even if there were evidence for the reliability of the authors of these texts with respect to the existence of natural entities and the occurrence of natural events, that would be negligible evidence in support of the claim that the authors are reliable with respect to the existence of non-natural entities and the occurrence of non-natural events. Moreover, typically, there is hardly any evidence that the authors are reliable in connection with the existence of natural entities and the occurrence of natural events. Sure, the texts sometimes refer to genuine historical events involving genuine historical figures in genuine historical locations. But that does not come close to establishing that the authors are reliable recorders of the existence of natural entities and the occurrence of natural events. What are missing from the historical record are multiple independent confirmations of detailed descriptions of the existence of natural entities and the occurrence of natural events – and the existence of non-natural entities and the occurrence of non-natural events – in central religious texts. Even where there are multiple detailed descriptions of entities and events in different central religious texts, we always have compelling evidence that the texts were not produced independently of one another.

There is nothing in the existence and content of central religious texts that favours theism over naturalism. Every best big picture says that almost all central religious texts, insofar as they are taken to be truth-assessable descriptions, are full of historical, moral, social, scientific, philosophical, and theological falsehoods. Every best big picture must explain the existence and content of all central religious texts. Best naturalistic big pictures have a uniform story to tell about all central religious texts. That leaves them very well positioned, and not in the least in need of engagement in the kind of special pleading characteristic of best theistic big pictures that claim support from the central texts of theistic religions.

3.10 Divination

Almost all religions involve alleged communication with gods: interpretation of omens, divination of future events, prayers and rituals that prompt divine intercession, and various kinds of conversation. Here, I shall consider only the case of divination.

The range of human divinatory practices is immense. Entities used for divination include: *chance artefacts* (e.g. cards, coins, and dice); *dangerous things* (e.g. arrows, needles, and swords); *environmental features* (e.g. clouds, flames, mountains, and stars); *human properties* (e.g. blood, gazing, and palms); *linguistic items* (e.g. books, handwriting, and overheard speech); *mathematical entities* (e.g. birthdates, fractals, and logarithms); *non-human living things* (e.g. beetles, flight, and urine); and *sacred things* (e.g. auras, idols, and saints).

But, of course, while almost anything can be adapted to the purposes of divination, most people who adopt divinatory practices cleave to a very small range. Moreover, in general, people who adopt particular divinatory practices are sceptical about the efficacy of other divinatory practices. Enthusiasm for divination by, for example, boiling the heads of donkeys, is highly localised.

There are no prizes for guessing what naturalists say about divination and about divine communication more broadly. Every best big picture says that no more than a vanishingly small fraction of claims to successful divinatory practices – and successful communication with gods – are true. Best naturalistic big pictures take a unified approach to all claims to successful divinatory practices: there are no successful divinatory practices, and there is no successful communication with gods. Competing best theistic big pictures which maintain that there are particular successful divinatory practices and particular successful means of communication with the gods are required to engage in special pleading on behalf of their favoured practices of divination and communication with the gods. In the absence of any demonstration, by methods to which all with relevant expertise agree, that there is a tiny fraction of privileged practices of divination and communication with gods that actually work, there is nothing in the data about divinatory practices and alleged communication with gods that creates any kind of explanatory disadvantage for best naturalistic big pictures.

3.11 Concluding Observations

The case for naturalism that I have sketched is a case for atheism. Not all atheists are naturalists; not all atheists will endorse this case. That's fine. Atheists who are not naturalists are free to mount other cases. However, I shall not attempt to present – or assess – any other cases for atheism here.

The case for atheism that I have presented has two main parts. The first part is a defence of the claim that best naturalistic big pictures are minimal: every best non-naturalistic big picture is committed to everything to which best naturalistic big pictures are committed and more besides. The second part is a defence of the claim that best naturalistic big pictures are maximal: there is nothing that is better explained by best non-naturalistic big pictures than by best naturalistic big pictures.

In the presentation here, the second part of the case is given a very quick sketch. At many points, I have argued only that best naturalistic big pictures are better than best theistic big pictures. Moreover, throughout, I have left many points of detail undiscussed. The aim of this sketch is *not* to convince those who do not already believe that best atheistic big pictures are the best big pictures. Rather, the aim is to indicate a set of considerations to which some atheists will appeal if they are asked to explain why they take themselves to be justified in believing as they do.

In closing, it may be worth adding a few further observations about the case that has been sketched.

The case that has been sketched restricts its attention to causal reality. The considerations addressed – causation, design, mind, anomaly, experience, scripture, and divination – are all concerned with descriptive, non-evaluative, non-normative domains. But big pictures are theories of everything; in addition to what they have to say about descriptive domains, big pictures also give accounts of evaluative and normative matters. Don't we need to consider what best atheistic big pictures say about evaluative and normative matters when we are deciding whether best atheistic big pictures are better than best theistic big pictures?

Not at all! The question in which we are interested – when we compare best atheistic big pictures with best theistic big pictures – is a purely descriptive question: *are there gods?* Questions about best evaluative and best normative views are simply independent of questions about best descriptive views. Of course, if there are gods, then the best evaluative and best normative views will apply to them, but there is no reason to suppose that the content of the best evaluative and best normative theories depends upon whether there are gods. Rather, the best atheistic big pictures and the best theistic big pictures will simply incorporate the best evaluative and the best normative views, and will apply those views to everything that they take to belong to the causal domain.

Of course, the claims that I have just made are controversial. Some theists suppose that, if there were no gods, there would be nothing evaluative or normative. More theists suppose that, if there were no gods, evaluative and normative matters would be fundamentally different from how they suppose that they actually are. I do not think that either of these views belongs to best theistic big pictures; I maintain instead that, if there are evaluative and normative truths, then fundamental evaluative and normative truths are both necessary and primitive. However, I shall leave argument about that for another occasion.

For different approaches to arguing for atheism, see: Everitt (2004), Le Poidevin (1996), Mackie (1982), Martin (1990), and Sobel (2004); for a more detailed exposition of my own approach, see Oppy (2013). For more discussion of explanations of the existence of our universe, see Goldschmidt (2013) and Reichenbach (2017); for more discussion of the alleged fine-tuning of our universe, see Friedrich (2017), Leslie (1989), and Manson (2003); for further discussion of explanations of mind-edness, see Smart (2007) and van Gulick (2014); for further discussion of miracles, see Dawes (2009), Earman (2000), Hajek (2008), and Millican (2013); for further discussion of religious experience, see Atran (2002), Guthrie (1993), James (1902), and Talmont-Kaminski (2012); and for further discussion of divination, see Smith (2017).

4 A Case for Preferring Agnosticism to Atheism

There are various common objections to agnosticism. Some people say that 'agnosticism' is just a label for atheists who are not willing to own up to their atheism. Some people say that 'agnosticism' is a label for those who – incoherently – seek a compromise position. Some people say that agnosticism is merely a pitiful, immoral, anti-intellectual state of indecision. Some people say that agnosticism is not really a serious alternative to atheism and theism; it is merely a halfway house for those who haven't yet made up their minds.

These common objections entirely miss the mark.

Agnostics are those who suspend judgement on the question whether there are gods. There is nothing that places agnosticism closer to atheism than to theism. So it is obviously not the case that 'agnostics' are atheists who are not willing to own up to their atheism. Perhaps it is true that some atheists call themselves 'agnostics'; but, if this is the case, it is much more likely to arise from confusion about the proper use of the terms 'atheist' and 'agnostic' than from an unwillingness to own up to being an atheist. After all, in circumstances in which one might be reluctant to own up to being an atheist, one would very likely also be unwilling to own up to being an agnostic.

There is nothing that marks out agnosticism as a compromise between atheism and theism. Atheists believe that there are no gods. Theists believe that there is at least one god. Agnostics neither believe that there are no gods nor believe that there is at least one god. Rather than being a compromise between atheism and theism, agnosticism is a rejection of both. Perhaps it might be objected that agnosticism is characterised by commitment to something like the claim that it is up in the air whether there are gods. But it isn't right to suppose that agnosticism is characterised by their attitude towards the claim that it is up in the air whether there are gods. It is perfectly possible to suppose that it is not up in the air whether there are gods while nonetheless being an agnostic: all one needs to suppose is that definitive news is still on its way about which of atheism and theism is the correct position to take up. The important feature of agnostics is that, having considered whether there are gods, agnostics suspend judgement. There is no further proposition that agnostics must believe in order to be agnostics.

It is obviously not true that all agnostics are immoral and anti-intellectual. Agnostics suspend judgement on the question whether there are gods, not on questions about morality, science, philosophy, and so forth. True enough, agnostics may well be committed to epistemological principles that enjoin suspension of judgement on questions other than whether there are gods. Perhaps, for example, an agnostic might suppose that one should proportion one's credence in a given proposition to the strength of the reasons that one has for taking that proposition to be true. But there is no good ground for supposing that a plausible epistemological principle of this kind enjoins any kind of wide-ranging scepticism. If you get a result to the contrary, then you are just making mistakes in your mapping from credences to all-or-nothing beliefs.

It is also obviously not true to say that agnosticism is a halfway house for those who have not yet made up their minds. Inhabitants of halfway houses are those who have not yet given attention to a sufficiently wide range of considerations; they may well shift their stances as they take more considerations into account. But there is nothing that makes it more likely that an inhabitant of a halfway house is an agnostic rather than an atheist or a theist. Agnostics who have given sufficiently sustained attention to a wide range of considerations are no more likely to change their stances than similarly placed atheists and theists.

4.1 Outline

A case for preferring agnosticism to atheism can be readily adapted from the case – made in the previous chapter – for preferring atheism to theism. The overall structure of the case is very similar. In particular, the case is in two parts. First, it is claimed that it is unclear whether best atheistic big pictures are more or less committing than best theistic big pictures. Second, it is claimed that it is unclear whether best atheistic big pictures have less or more explanatory breadth and depth than best theistic big pictures. Given that it is unclear whether best atheistic big pictures are more or less committing than best theistic big pictures, and that it is also unclear whether best atheistic big pictures have less or more explanatory breadth and depth than best theistic big pictures, it is unclear whether best atheistic big pictures are better or worse than best theistic big pictures. But, if it is unclear whether best atheistic big pictures are better or worse than best theistic big pictures, then it is unclear whether to prefer atheism to theism or to prefer theism to atheism. Which is just to say that we suspend judgement on the question whether there are gods.

4.2 Minimality

Suppose we grant that best naturalistic big pictures are minimal in the class of best big pictures. Even so, it does not follow that other best atheistic big pictures are less committing than best theistic big pictures. True enough, best theistic big pictures are committed to everything to which best naturalistic big pictures are committed, and more besides. But this is also true for all best atheistic big pictures that are not best naturalistic big pictures: these, too, are committed to everything to which best naturalistic big pictures are committed, and more besides.

It may be that, when we compare other best atheistic big pictures with best theistic big pictures, we end up suspending judgement on the question whether other best atheistic big pictures are more or less committing than best theistic big pictures. Perhaps, for example, when we compare particular best non-naturalistic atheistic big pictures with best theistic big pictures, we have no way of weighing the additional commitments to entities, kinds of entities, properties, kinds of properties, basic principles, and kinds of basic principles. If, for example, there are more kinds of new entities but fewer kinds of new properties in best non-naturalistic atheistic big pictures, then we may see no alternative to suspending judgement on the question whether best non-naturalistic atheistic big pictures are more or less committing than best theistic big pictures.

Given the vast extent of our ignorance, it does not seem unreasonable to suspend judgement on the question whether best non-naturalistic atheistic big pictures are more or less committing than best theistic big pictures. If there are more things in heaven and earth than are dreamed of in best naturalistic big pictures, then it is hard to see how to rule out the claim that best big pictures that include or entail the claim that there is at least one god are no more theoretically committing than best big pictures that include or entail the claim that there are no gods.

4.3 Maximality

The core of the case for agnosticism is that it is unclear whether best atheistic big pictures have more or less explanatory breadth and depth than best theistic big pictures. There are two parts to the case. First, we argue that it is unclear whether best naturalistic big pictures have more or less explanatory breadth than best theistic big pictures. Second, we argue that it is unclear whether any other best atheistic big pictures have more or less explanatory breadth and depth than best theistic big pictures. In our discussion, we shall focus on the first part of this case.

Our discussion of the question whether best naturalistic big pictures have more or less explanatory breadth than best theistic big pictures itself divides into two parts. One question is whether, on the various data points that were considered in the earlier case for atheism, we do better to suspend judgement on the claim that best naturalistic big pictures have no less explanatory breadth and depth than best theistic big pictures. Another question is whether we do better to suspend judgement on the claim that consideration of further data points would make no difference to the strength of the earlier case for atheism. In our discussion, we shall focus our attention on the first question.

4.4 Causation

In the case for preferring atheism to theism, it was argued that best atheistic big pictures do not give better ultimate explanations than best naturalistic big pictures of the existence of causal reality. Each possible ultimate explanation – brute contingency, brute necessity, infinite regress – fits at least as well with best naturalistic big pictures as it does with best theistic big pictures. For example, according to this line of thought, there is no respect in which the claim that God exists of necessity is more theoretically virtuous than the claim that natural reality exists of necessity.

But perhaps you might wonder whether this is really so. Might it be, for example, that God is a better candidate than natural reality to be a necessary existent? Might it be that, while there is at least some sense that attaches to the claim that God exists of necessity, there just is no sense that attaches to the claim that natural reality exists of necessity? If you are unsure whether it makes sense to suppose that natural reality exists of necessity, even though it does make sense to suppose that God exists of necessity, they you will be unsure whether there is reason to suppose that best theistic big pictures afford a better explanation than best naturalistic big pictures of the existence of causal reality.

Moreover, given that there is no expert consensus on the question whether it makes sense to suppose that natural reality exists of necessity, you might take that lack of expert consensus as further reason for suspension of judgement: perhaps it would be imprudent to suppose that it makes just as much sense to maintain that natural reality exists of necessity as it does to maintain that God exists of necessity, given that there is no expert consensus on this matter.

4.5 Design

The case that was made for the claim that there is no difference in the ultimate explanation of cosmic fine-tuning by best naturalistic big pictures and best theistic big pictures depended upon the claim that there is just as much that is taken as primitive in best theistic big pictures, in connection with cosmic fine-tuning, as there is in best naturalistic big pictures. Where best naturalistic big pictures suppose that fixing of the values of the adjustable parameters is brutely contingent, best theistic big pictures suppose that fixing of divine preferences for the values of these parameters is brutely contingent.

But perhaps you might wonder whether this is really so. In particular, you might wonder whether there is a greater range for the possible values of the parameters in best naturalistic big pictures than in best theistic big pictures. On best naturalistic big pictures, any assignment of values to the adjustable parameters characterises a family of possible universes. Similarly, on best theistic big pictures, any assignment of preferences for the values of the adjustable parameters characterises a family of possible universes. But could it be that there are constraints on the assignment of divine preferences for the values of the adjustable parameters that have no counterpart in the assignment of values to the adjustable parameters themselves? If there is a much larger class of possibilities countenanced in best naturalistic big pictures than in best theistic big pictures, then there is some temptation to think that best theistic big pictures give a better explanation of the values that the adjustable parameters actually take: that the adjustable parameters take these values is more likely on best theistic big pictures than on best naturalistic big pictures.

Perhaps you might also wonder whether there *could be* constraints on the assignment of divine preferences for the values of the adjustable parameters that have no counterpart in the assignment of values to the adjustable parameters themselves. Given that there is a range of preferences that the gods could have, and given that there is nothing that explains why the gods have the particular preferences that they have *rather than* other preferences that they might have had, what could explain the constraint upon their preferences? Why, in particular, should it be that the gods are *unable* to make universes that are either very short-lived or else explode so rapidly that they always consist of more or less nothing but empty space?

In view of the significant uncertainties here – and bearing in mind that there is no expert consensus on these matters – it seems that one might well reasonably come to suspension of judgement: perhaps it is imprudent to believe that there is just as much that is taken as primitive in best theistic big pictures, in connection with cosmic fine-tuning, as there is in best naturalistic big pictures, and suitably prudent rather to suspend judgement on the question whether there is just as much that is taken as primitive in best theistic big pictures, in connection with cosmic fine-tuning, as there is in best naturalistic big pictures.

4.6 Mind

In the case for preferring atheism to theism, it was argued that considerations about mindedness do not favour best theistic theories over best naturalistic theories. In particular, it was argued that, in order to explain the various aspects of the mindedness of organisms, we need appeal only to biological processes in those organisms, the local environments of those organisms, and the local social and biological evolutionary histories of those organisms. For minded organisms to be conscious just is for them to be engaged in certain kinds of neural processing. And for minded organisms to be perceiving their immediate environments just is for them, in those environments, to be engaged in certain kinds of neural processing that have been appropriately shaped by local, social, and evolutionary history, and that are appropriately causally related to those environments.

You might wonder whether this is so. Moreover, you might wonder whether the earlier responses to possible objections to this claim are really adequate. There is a vast range of opinion on 'the mind/body problem' and the other topics – cosmic justice, immortality, 'the hard problem of consciousness', and the evolution of our reasoning capacities – taken up in those previously considered objections. Of course, not every alternative to the 'identity theory' creates problems for the earlier argument. If, for example, the best big pictures are committed to the kind of panpsychism that Chalmers (1996) favours – wherein even electrons have proto-consciousness – we can simply amend the account of best naturalistic big pictures by adding a commitment to proto-consciousness, and carrying on as before. However, in view of the widespread debate about these matters, it may be that we do better to suspend judgement on the question whether best naturalistic big pictures give an explanation of mindedness that is in no way inferior to explanations given in best theistic big pictures.

4.7 Anomaly

The case for the claim that considerations about miracles do not favour best theistic big pictures over best naturalistic big pictures was based on consideration of the range of reports of anomalous entities and events within and without religions. However, even if you accept that the range of reports of anomalous entities and events within and without religions casts doubt on the suggestion that miracle reports favour best theistic big pictures over best naturalistic big pictures, you might still wonder whether other considerations about miracles favour best theistic big pictures over best naturalistic big pictures.

Suppose that *you* have undergone an anomalous experience of a kind that some others are disposed to interpret as evidence for the occurrence of a miracle. Perhaps, for example, while walking alone in a field, you hear a voice telling you to become a Rastafarian, despite the fact that there is no one around who could be speaking to you. If this kind of thing happens to you only once, you might – eventually – dismiss it as some kind of hallucination. And if this kind of thing happens to you frequently, you will likely end up undergoing extensive medical tests to try to determine the nature of the psychological disorder from which you evidently suffer. But if this kind of thing happens to you more than once, with suitable infrequency – say, no more than once every five or six years – then you might come to have some doubts about whether you'd do best to dismiss the idea that you are receiving a message from the gods. True enough, lots of people who hear voices have psychological disorders; true enough, we have very good reason to think that almost everyone who hears voices would do best not to believe what the voices tell them (unless they already and independently have sufficient reason to believe those things). But, if our case is special in the right kinds of ways, then maybe – *maybe* – we have some reason to suspend judgement on the question whether we have evidence that there are gods.

It is not uncommon for non-believers to be asked what it would take to convince them to adopt particular religious beliefs. While it is hard to know what to say in response to this question – other than to say that those who already believe are likely better placed to answer it, drawing upon their own experience – it happens not infrequently that non-believers suggest some variant of the example that I have been discussing. One way to strengthen the example is to have multitudes undergo the same experience at the same time; rather than have me walking alone in a field, make it that I am with a large group who are walking together in the field, and let the voice boom down from the sky (so that trickery on the part of some members of the group is plainly ruled out). Perhaps it is plausible to suppose that this kind of case would provide reason to suspend judgement on the question whether there are gods, or even to believe that there are gods, for those who are part of the group. (Of course, it is a separate question – already covered in our previous discussion – whether anyone who has not actually been part of such a group has any reason to believe that there have been episodes like this.)

4.8 Experience

The case for the claim that considerations about religious experience do not favour best theistic big pictures over best naturalistic big pictures was based on considerations about the content and provenance of mystical experience. Given that mystical experience has negligible communicable content, given that mystical experience is very often generated by conditions that are correlated with poor performance on even quite simple cognitive tasks, and given that mystical experience is common to all religious – and non-religious – traditions, it is hard to accept that reports of mystical experience favour best theistic big pictures over best naturalistic big pictures.

But what if you are, yourself, someone who regularly undergoes mystical experiences? And what if you find yourself conflicted in your attitude towards these mystical experiences? On the one hand, you find yourself somewhat disposed towards believing that they are an indication that there is 'something more' than the world that is disclosed in regular perceptual experience. But, on the other hand, you also take seriously the considerations about the general lack of content and questionable provenance of mystical experience. Your 'unitive' experiences of evanescence, ineffability, passivity, and tranquillity *might* be indications of 'something more', but they might also be mere 'noise' that is explained away by mature cognitive science and evolutionary theory. On balance, you might suppose that you do best to suspend judgement on the question whether mystical experience does provide some evidence that there are gods.

Even if you are not, yourself, someone who has ever undergone a mystical experience, you might find yourself a bit conflicted in your attitude towards mystical experiences. Sure, given that mystical experiences are reported across all religious – and non-religious – traditions, there is good reason to doubt that reports of mystical experience support any particular religious tradition. But that leaves it open whether reports of mystical experience provide some evidence that there are gods. You might suspend judgement on the question whether reports of mystical experience provide some evidence that there are gods, while nonetheless being relatively certain that reports of mystical experience do not support any claims about the existence of *particular* gods.

4.9 Scripture

The case for the claim that considerations about central religious texts do not support best theistic big pictures over best naturalistic big pictures was based on a range of observations about the uncertainties involved in dating the initial composition and subsequent redaction of these texts, the barriers to confident interpretation of these texts, the historical reliability of the authors of these texts, and so forth. Given the many similarities between central religious texts across different religions, it is hard to accept that the existence and content of central religious texts favour best theistic big pictures over best naturalistic big pictures.

But what if you are particularly knowledgeable about the religious texts that belong to one particular religion and you find yourself conflicted in your attitude towards those religious texts? Why can't it be that you find yourself disposed to suspend judgement about the merits of those texts, particularly given local disputes that focus on the merits of just those texts? True enough, you may recognise that there is something parochial about your focus on just those texts – but it is not obvious that that consideration is sufficient to move you from suspension of judgement to outright disbelief.

4.10 Divination

In the cases considered so far – causation, design, mind, anomaly, experience, and scripture – I have suggested that it might not be unreasonable for agnostics to suspend judgement on the question whether best naturalistic big pictures have greater explanatory breadth and depth than best theistic big pictures in connection with the relevant data.

I think that, in connection with the data concerning divination, it is not very plausible to suppose that agnostics suspend judgement on the question whether best naturalistic big pictures have greater explanatory breadth and depth than best theistic big pictures. Rather, agnostics should suppose that best naturalistic big pictures and best theistic big pictures *agree* in their explanation of the data: best theistic big pictures give the same explanation of the data that is given by best naturalistic big pictures.

There is nothing that requires theists to believe that there are successful divinatory practices; it is perfectly open to theists to deny that any divinatory practices provide information about future events. Agnostics should suppose that best theistic big pictures deny that any divinatory practices provide information about future events.

4.11 Concluding Observations

There are various pieces to put together in the construction of a case for preferring agnosticism to atheism.

Given that we accept the methodology set out earlier – i.e. given that we accept that, in identifying best big pictures, we consider the trade-off between minimising theoretical commitments and maximising explanatory breadth and depth – the case for preferring agnosticism to atheism lies in the claim that there are too many uncertainties in the assessment to allow us to form the judgement that best atheistic big pictures are better – or worse – than best theistic big pictures.

One important question is whether we can be confident that best atheistic big pictures are best naturalistic big pictures. Even if we can be fairly confident that best naturalistic big pictures have fewer theoretical commitments than any other best big pictures, it may not be obvious that best atheistic big pictures have fewer theoretical commitments than best theistic big pictures. If we have sufficient reasons for suspending judgement on the question whether best naturalistic big pictures are among the best big pictures, then we may have sufficient reasons for suspending judgement on the question whether best atheistic big pictures have fewer theoretical commitments than best theistic big pictures.

The other important question is whether we can be confident in our weighing of the explanatory breadth and depth of best atheistic big pictures and best theistic big pictures. So long as there are enough domains on which we cannot be confident in our weighing of the explanatory breadth and depth of best atheistic big pictures and best theistic big pictures, we shall have reason for suspending judgement on the question whether best atheistic big pictures are better than best theistic big pictures. In the preceding discussion, we have considered the prospects for raising doubts about whether best naturalistic big pictures do at least as well as best theistic big pictures in explaining data concerning causation, design, mind, anomaly, experience, and scripture. I have suggested that there may be some reasons for doubt that arise in connection with each of these domains.

Apart from the uncertainties already canvassed, an agnostic might also take it to be uncertain whether there are other domains – not considered in the preceding discussion – on which best atheistic big pictures fail to have greater explanatory breadth and depth than best theistic big pictures; an agnostic might also take it to be uncertain whether the methodology that we set out earlier really is the right way to think about assessing the relative merits of atheism and theism.

Given the complexity of the task of assessing best atheistic big pictures and best theistic big pictures – and given the wide range of expert opinion about the outcome of this assessment – it seems plausible to claim that agnosticism is rationally permissible. That is, it seems plausible to claim that suspension of judgement can be a rational response to the question whether there are gods, on the part of those who consider the matter with sufficient diligence, intelligence, energy, and so forth. Just as the case sketched in the preceding chapter is best taken as an example of the kind of response that thoughtful, intelligent, well-informed atheists can make when asked to explain why they believe as they do, so too the case sketched in the present chapter is best taken as an indication of the kind of response that thoughtful, intelligent, well-informed agnostics can make when asked to explain why they believe as they do.

What is my own view? While I think that atheism, agnosticism, and theism are all rationally permissible, I am an atheist: when I make the best evaluation that I can of all of the relevant considerations, I come down on the side of the claim that there are no gods. But I do not suppose that all sufficiently thoughtful, intelligent, and well-informed people will – or must – agree with me in this judgement. When we consider the best cases for atheism, agnosticism and theism, there are many, many points where we are required to make judgements; and it is the accumulation of those many, many judgements that feeds into our overall assessment.

For differing approaches to arguing for agnosticism, see Draper (2017), Huxley (1889/1894), Le Poidevin (2010), and Schellenberg (2007).

Bibliography

Allen, W. (1964) *Woody Allen* Colpix CP 518 (track eight: 'NYU').
Antony, L. (ed.) (2007) *Philosophers without Gods.* Oxford: Oxford University Press.
Atran, S. (2002) *In Gods We Trust.* New York: Oxford University Press.
Ayer, A. (1936) *Logic, Truth and Language.* London: Victor Gollancz Ltd.
Berman, D. (1988) *A History of Atheism in Britain.* Abingdon: Routledge.
Blom, P. (2010) *A Wicked Company: The Forgotten Radicalism of the European Enlightenment.* New York: Basic Books.
Bonett, W. (ed.) (2010) *The Australian Book of Atheism.* Melbourne: Scribe.
Budd, S. (1977) *Varieties of Unbelief: Atheists and Agnostics in English Society 1850–1960.* Portsmouth: Heinemann.
Bullivant, S. (2013) 'Defining "Atheism"' in Bullivant and Ruse, 11–21.
Bullivant, S. and Ruse, M. (eds.) (2013) *Handbook of Atheism.* Oxford: Oxford University Press.
Chalmers, D. (1996) *The Conscious Mind.* Oxford: Oxford University Press.
Cline, A. (2016) 'University Study on American Attitudes towards Atheists' *ThoughtCo,* www.thoughtco.com/study-american-attitudes-towards-atheists-248478
Colbert, S. (2007) *I am America (and So Can You!).* New York: Grand Central Publishing.
Curran, M. (2012) *Atheism, Religion and Enlightenment in Pre-Revolutionary Europe.* London: Boydell & Brewer.
Dawes, G. (2009) *Theism and Explanation.* New York: Routledge.
D'Holbach, P. (1790/1820) *The System of Nature,* translated by S. Wilkinson. London: Thomas Davison.
Doyle, A. (1922/2006) *The Coming of the Fairies.* Lincoln: University of Nebraska Press.
Draper, P. (2017) 'Atheism and Agnosticism' *Stanford Encyclopedia of Philosophy,* https://plato.stanford.edu/entries/atheism-agnosticism/
Drum, K. (2017) 'Atheists Open Gap against Muslims for Title of most Hated Religious Group in America' *Mother Jones,* www.motherjones.com/kevin-drum/2017/02/atheists-no-longer-most-hated-religious-group-america/
Earman, J. (1996) *Bayes or Bust?* Cambridge: MIT Press.

Earman, J. (2000) *Hume's Abject Failure*. Oxford: Oxford University Press.

Edgell, P., Gerteis, J., and Hartmann, D. (2006) 'Atheists as "Other": Moral Boundaries and Cultural Membership in American Society' *American Sociological Review* 71, 211–34.

Everitt, N. (2004) *The Non-Existence of God*. London: Routledge.

Flynn, T. (ed.) (2007) *The New Encyclopedia of Unbelief*. Amherst: Prometheus.

Forbes, G. (1994) *Modern Logic*. Oxford: Oxford University Press.

Friedrich, S. (2017) 'Fine-Tuning' *Stanford Encyclopaedia of Philosophy*, https://plato.stanford.edu/entries/fine-tuning/

Gervais, W. and Najile, M. (2017) 'How Many Atheists are There?' *Social Psychological and Personality Science*, DOI: 10.1177/1948550617707015.

Gervais, W., Norenzayan, A., and Shariff, A. (2011) 'Do you Believe in Atheists? Distrust is Central to Anti-Atheist Prejudice' *Journal of Personality and Social Psychology* 101: 1189–206.

Goldschmidt, T. (ed.) (2013) *The Puzzle of Existence*. London: Routledge.

Griffiths, F. and Lynch, C. (2009) *Reflections on the Cottingley Fairies*. Black Hawk: JMJ Publications.

Guthrie, S. (1993) *Faces in the Clouds*. New York: Oxford University Press.

Hájek, A. (2008) 'Are Miracles Chimerical?' *Oxford Studies in Philosophy of Religion* 1: 82–104.

Haldeman-Julius, E. (1931) *The Meaning of Atheism*. Girard: Haldeman-Julius Publications.

Hirschberg, D. (n.d.) Quote available at http://atheisme.free.fr/Quotes/Atheist.htm.

Horwich, P. (1982) *Probability and Evidence*. Cambridge: Cambridge University Press.

Hunter, M. and Wootton, D. (eds.) (1992) *Atheism from the Reformation to the Enlightenment*. Oxford: Clarendon.

Huxley, T. (1889/1894) 'Agnosticism and Christianity' in *Collected Essays of Thomas Henry Huxley, Volume 5*. Cambridge: Cambridge University Press, 309–65.

Jacoby, S. (2013) *The Great Agnostic: Robert Ingersoll and American Free Thought*. New Haven: Yale University Press.

James, W. (1902) *Varieties of Religious Experience*. London: Longmans.

Jillette, P. (2011) *God, No!: Signs You May Already be an Atheist and Other Magical Tales* New York: Simon & Schuster.

Korzdorfer, N. (2009) 'Brad Pitt Interview: "With Six Kids Each Morning it is About Surviving"', *Bild.com*, www.bild.de/news/bild-english/inglourious-basterd-star-on-angelina-jolie-and-six-kids-9110388.bild.html.

Le Poidevin, R. (1996) *Arguing for Atheism*. London: Routledge.

Le Poidevin, R. (2010) *Agnosticism*. Oxford: Oxford University Press.

Leslie, J. (1989) *Universes*. London: Routledge.

Losure, M. (2012) *The Fairy Ring; or Elise and Frances Fool the World*. Somerville: Candlewick Press.

Manson, N. (ed.) (2003) *God and Design*. London: Routledge.

Mackie, J. (1982) *The Miracle of Theism*. Oxford: Clarendon.

Martin, M. (1990) *Atheism: A Philosophical Justification*. Philadelphia: Temple University Press.

Martin, M. (ed.) (2007) *Companion to Atheism*. Cambridge: Cambridge University Press.

McCarthy, J. (2007) 'Religion as a Theory' *Internet Archive*, https://web.archive.org/web/20131004213311/http://www-formal.stanford.edu/jmc/commentary.html.

Millican, P. (2013) 'Twenty Questions about Hume's "Of Miracles"' in A. O'Hear (ed.) *Philosophy and Religion*. Cambridge: Cambridge University Press, 151–92.

Ohlheiser, A. (2013) 'There are 13 Countries where Atheism is Punishable by Death' *The Atlantic* www.theatlantic.com/international/archive/2013/12/13-countries-where-atheism-punishable-death/355961/

Oppy, G. (2013) *The Best Argument against God*. London: Palgrave Macmillan.

Oppy, G. (ed.) (2018) *A Companion to Atheism and Philosophy*. Chichester: Wiley-Blackwell.

Paul, G. (2005) 'Cross-National Correlations of Quantifiable Societal Health with Popular Religiosity and Secularism in Prosperous Democracies' *Journal of Religion and Society* 7: 1–17.

Phipps, S. (2013) 'Should we Care Whether God exists?' *Nooga.com*, http://nooga.com/164154/apatheism-should-we-care-whether-god-exists/

Platinga, A. (2012) *Where the Conflict Really Lies* Oxford: Oxford University Press

Priest, G. (2000) *Logic: A Very Short Introduction*. Oxford: Oxford University Press.

Rauch, J. (2003) 'Let it Be: Three Cheers for Apatheism' *The Atlantic Monthly*, www.theatlantic.com/magazine/archive/2003/05/let-it-be/302726/

Reichenbach, B. (2017) 'Cosmological Argument' *Stanford Encyclopaedia of Philosophy*, https://plato.stanford.edu/entries/cosmological-argument/

Reppert, V. (2009) 'The Argument from Reason in W. Craig and J. Moreland (eds.) Companion to Natural Theology Maldon: Wiley-Blackwell

Roberts, S. (n.d.) 'Brief History of the Quote', *Freelink,* http://freelink .wildlink.com/quote_history.php.

Rowe, W. (1976) 'The Ontological Argument and Begging the Question' *International Journal for Philosophy of Religion* 7: 443–7.

Sartre, J. (1964) *The Words,* translated by B. Frechtman. New York: George Braziller.

Schellenberg, J. (2007) *The Wisdom to Doubt: A Justification of Religious Scepticism.* Ithaca: Cornell University Press.

Shapiro, S. (2013) 'Classical Logic' *Stanford Encyclopedia of Philosophy,* https://plato.stanford.edu/entries/logic-classical/

Sheard, M. (2014) 'Ninety-Eight Atheists: Atheism among the Non-Elite in Twentieth Century Britain' *Secularism and Non-Religion,* https://secu larismandnonreligion.org/articles/10.5334/snr.ar/

Smart, J. (2007) 'The Mind/Brain Identity Theory' *Stanford Encyclopaedia of Philosophy,* https://plato.stanford.edu/entries/mind-identity/

Smith, T. (2017) *Science and Religion: A Conflict of Methods.* PhD dissertation, University of Otago.

Sobel, J. (2004) *Logic and Theism.* Cambridge: Cambridge University Press.

Swinburne, R. (ed.) (2002) *Bayes' Theorem.* Oxford: Oxford University Press.

Talbott, W. (2008) 'Bayesian Epistemology' *Stanford Encyclopaedia of Philosophy,* https://plato.stanford.edu/entries/epistemology-bayesian/

Talmont-Kaminski, K. (2012) *In a Mirror Darkly.* Lublin: Wydawnictwo Uniwersytetu Marii Curie-Skłodowskiej.

Thrower, J. (2000) *Western Atheism: A Short History.* Amherst: Prometheus.

Van Gulick, R. (2014) 'Consciousness' *Stanford Encyclopaedia of Philosophy,* https://plato.stanford.edu/entries/consciousness/

Van Inwagen, P. (2018) 'Begging the Question' in G. Oppy (ed.) *Ontological Arguments.* Cambridge: Cambridge University Press.

Von Hegner, I. (2016) 'Gods and Dictatorships: A Defence of Heroic Apatheism' *Science, Religion and Culture* 3.

Whitmarsh, T. (2015) *Battling Gods: Atheism in the Ancient World.* New York: Knopf.

Zuckerman, P. (2009) 'Atheism, Secularity and Well-Being: How the Findings of Social Science Counter Negative Stereotypes and Assumptions' *Sociology Compass* 3: 949–71.

Printed in the United States
By Bookmasters